KEY

EVIDENCE

BEVERLEY HOPKINS

Hodder & Stoughton

A MEMBER OF THE HODDER HEADLINE GROUP

Orders: please contact Bookpoint Ltd, 130 Milton Park, Abingdon, Oxon OX14 4SB.
Telephone: (44) 01235 827720. Fax: (44) 01235 400454. Lines are open from 9.00–6.00,
Monday to Saturday, with a 24-hour message answering service. You can also order through our
website www.hodderheadline.co.uk

British Library Cataloguing in Publication Data
A catalogue record for this title is available from The British Library.

ISBN 0 340 85935 0

First published 2003
Impression number   10 9 8 7 6 5 4 3 2 1
Year   2007 2006 2005 2004 2003

Typeset by Transet Limited, Leamington Spa, Warwickshire.
Printed in Great Britain for Hodder & Stoughton Educational, a division of Hodder Headline,
338 Euston Road, London NW1 3BH by Cox & Wyman Ltd, Reading, Berkshire.

CONTENTS

PREFACE

The Key Facts series is designed to give a clear view of each subject. This will be useful to students when tackling new topics and is invaluable as a revision aid. Most chapters open with an outline in diagram form of the points covered in that chapter. The points are then developed in list form to make learning easier. Supporting cases are given throughout by name and for some complex areas the facts of cases are given to reinforce the point being made.

Most Evidence examinations will require you to demonstrate your skills in applying the rules to fact scenarios. That requires a sound knowledge of case law because, although some rules are established through legislation, it is the case law that evolves around that legislation which often determines how the rules will be applied. This book aims to review each of the major rules of Evidence with the forthcoming examinations in mind. It incorporates all the important cases that either establish or impact upon the application of the rules, and includes some useful tips for handling complex areas such as the *Turnbull* rules on identification evidence, hearsay and similar fact evidence. In terms of depth, the book aims to condense the essential materials to facilitate revision, at the same time retaining sufficient detail to foster understanding of topics that have traditionally proved problematic for students.

LIST OF CASES

CHAPTER 1

INTRODUCTORY MATTERS

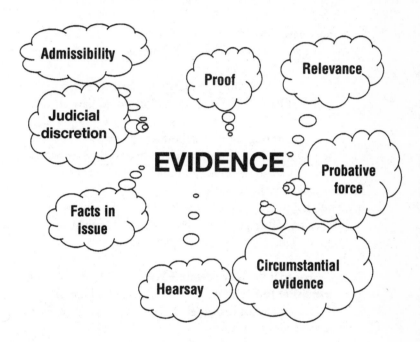

1.1 INTRODUCTION

This first introductory chapter deals with the preliminaries: important definitions, the distinction between relevance and admissibility and the nature of judicial discretion. Finally, it focuses briefly on human rights, identifying those rules of evidence which are most likely to be affected by the Human Rights Act 1998.

1.2 THE ROLE OF JUDGE AND JURY

1. In a criminal trial at Crown Court, judges are responsible for deciding matters of law and ensuring that trials are conducted fairly.
2. Judges have discretion to exclude admissible evidence:
   (a) at common law (because its prejudicial effect outweighs its probative value) and
   (b) under s78(1) Police and Criminal Evidence Act (PACE) 1984 where its admission would have such an adverse effect on the fairness of the proceedings that the court ought not to admit it.
3. The judge is obliged to sum up the case to the jury at the conclusion of the evidence, reminding them of the facts and directing them on the law.
4. The jury's responsibility is to decide questions of fact. The assessment of weight, the probative force of evidence, and the credibility of witnesses are primarily matters for the jury.
5. In a civil trial the judge assumes responsibility for deciding questions of law and fact. In the absence of a jury, there is no requirement for the judge to sum up the facts or to offer directions on the law.

1.3 WHAT IS EVIDENCE?

In a criminal trial, evidence is the means by which the prosecution tries to prove its case and the defendant tries to cast doubt upon the prosecution's evidence. Similarly, in a civil case, it is through adducing evidence that the claimant attempts to prove his case and the defendant attempts to counter the claimant's case.

1. **Testimony** is the most common form of evidence, whereby a witness tells the court what he has seen, heard etc. in his

own words. He will then be cross-examined in order that the testimony can be assessed.

2. **Documentary evidence** is admissible in certain circumstances, although oral testimony is generally preferred. Documentary evidence includes films, tapes, video recordings etc. Documentary evidence is a form of 'real evidence'.

3. **Real evidence** is normally something tangible that is produced for inspection by the court, such as the murder weapon; an intangible form of real evidence would be a viewing of the scene of an incident by the tribunal of fact.

1.4 THE CONCEPTS OF ADMISSIBILITY AND RELEVANCE

1. Evidence is admissible if it is receivable by the court.

2. It is a precondition for admissibility that evidence is **relevant** (*R v Turner* (1975)). A court may reject evidence because it is irrelevant, or insufficiently relevant to the facts in issue.

3. Relevant evidence is that which makes the fact requiring proof more or less probable. It was defined by Lord Simon of Glaisdale in *DPP v Kilbourne* (1973) in the following terms: 'Evidence is relevant if it is logically probative or disprobative of some matter which requires proof.'

1.4.1 Admissibility

Only three types of evidence are admissible:

1. **Facts in issue**
    (a) In a criminal case, the facts in issue are those facts that the prosecution must prove in order to establish the guilt of the defendant, together with those facts raised by way of defence that the prosecution must normally disprove.

(b) In a civil case, the facts in issue are those facts that the claimant must prove in order to establish his case, together with those facts that the defendant must prove to establish a defence, for example contributory negligence or *volenti*.

(c) What facts are in issue in any case will therefore depend upon the substantive law that is applicable and any defence that is raised.

2. **Facts relevant to a fact in issue:** otherwise known as **circumstantial evidence**.

(a) This is evidence from which an inference needs to be drawn by the tribunal of fact (judge, jury or bench of magistrates, depending upon the nature and mode of trial) before a fact in issue is proved.

(b) A fact is relevant to a fact in issue if its existence makes proof or disproof of a fact in issue more likely (see examples of circumstantial evidence at section 1.5 below).

3. **Collateral facts** relate to a witness rather than directly to the facts in issue; an eyewitness may, for example, be asked questions to establish whether he has good or poor vision.

Note: Any evidence which does not fall into one of the above three categories is **irrelevant** and **inadmissible**.

1.5 CLASSIFICATIONS OF EVIDENCE

1. **Direct evidence** is testimony that relates to the direct perception of a fact in issue, for example 'I saw him stab her with a pair of scissors'.

2. **Circumstantial evidence** is evidence from which an inference needs to be drawn by the tribunal of fact before a fact in issue is proved. Circumstantial evidence requires the tribunal of fact to decide:

(i) whether the relevant facts, or some of them, are proved, and if so

(ii) whether the fact in issue should be inferred from the existence of those facts.

An example of circumstantial evidence would be: 'I saw the accused running from the area where the body of the deceased was found. He was holding a blood-stained knife.' The jury would need to decide, firstly, whether they believed that evidence; and, secondly, whether they could infer from that evidence that the accused had killed the deceased.

3. **Primary evidence** is the best evidence there can be of a fact, for example the original contract as opposed to a photocopy.

4. **Secondary evidence** indicates that better evidence exists, so the photocopied contract would be secondary evidence.

5. **Insufficient evidence** is evidence that is so weak that no reasonable person could decide an issue in reliance upon that evidence alone.

6. *Prima facie* evidence is sufficient to prove a fact in the absence of any contradictory evidence.

7. A *voir dire* may also be referred to as a 'trial within a trial'. This is a procedure used to determine, for example, the competence of a witness to testify, or the admissibility of a disputed confession. In trials on indictment, a *voir dire* is normally held in the absence of the jury.

1.6 JUDICIAL DISCRETION

1. Under many of the 'rules', judges are given the responsibility of making judgements, for example weighing the probative value of evidence against its prejudicial effect.

2. Under s78(1) PACE 1984, judges have a statutory duty to ensure the fairness of criminal trials by excluding: 'any evidence on which the prosecution proposes to rely... if it appears to the court that, having regard to all the

circumstances, including the circumstances in which the evidence was obtained, the admission of the evidence would have such an adverse effect on the fairness of the proceedings that the court ought not to admit it.'

3. The s78(1) discretion may be used to exclude an otherwise admissible confession, identification evidence or any other prosecution evidence in the interests of fairness.

4. There is no corresponding 'inclusionary' discretion to include inadmissible evidence in the interests of fairness (*Sparks v R* (1964)).

5. Neither is there a general discretion to exclude relevant evidence adduced by the defence on the grounds of fairness.

1.7 THE HUMAN RIGHTS ACT 1998 (HRA 1998)

The coming into force of the HRA 1998 in October 2000 has paved the way for a number of challenges involving rules of evidence. The most obvious areas relate to:

1. reverse burdens of proof (where legislation imposes a legal burden of proof on a defendant in relation to a specific defence (see section 2.6))

2. the exercise of judicial discretion to exclude under s78 PACE 1984 (see section 12.1.3) and

3. the prohibition upon defendants cross-examining complainants in sexual cases upon previous sexual acts under s41 of the Youth Justice and Criminal Evidence Act 1999 (see section 4.8).

1.7.1 Article 6

The potential impact of the HRA 1998 is assessed at various stages throughout this book. The most relevant of the rights protected by the HRA 1998 is under Article 6, the right to a fair trial. Article 6(1) covers trials 'determining civil rights and obligations' as well as criminal charges. Article 6 guarantees:

(a) a fair and public hearing within a reasonable time by an independent and impartial tribunal;
(b) the presumption of innocence until guilt is established;
(c) certain minimum rights including:
    (i) the right to be informed of the nature of the charge;
    (ii) adequate time and facilities to prepare a defence;
    (iii) the right to legal assistance;
    (iv) the right to examine opposing witnesses;
    (v) the assistance of an interpreter where necessary.

Note: The case of *Neumeister v Austria* (1979–80) developed the concept of **equality of arms**: 'Each party must be afforded a reasonable opportunity to present his case … under conditions that do not place him at a substantial disadvantage vis a vis his opponent.' This principle has particular relevance to disclosure requirements (see section 14.2).

CHAPTER 2

THE BURDEN AND STANDARD OF PROOF

2.1 THE BURDEN OF PROOF IN CRIMINAL CASES

The legal and evidential burdens at various stages of a criminal trial

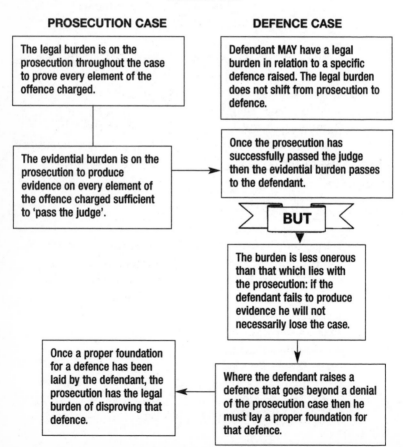

PROSECUTION CASE

The legal burden is on the prosecution throughout the case to prove every element of the offence charged.

The evidential burden is on the prosecution to produce evidence on every element of the offence charged sufficient to 'pass the judge'.

DEFENCE CASE

Defendant MAY have a legal burden in relation to a specific defence raised. The legal burden does not shift from prosecution to defence.

Once the prosecution has successfully passed the judge then the evidential burden passes to the defendant.

BUT

The burden is less onerous than that which lies with the prosecution: if the defendant fails to produce evidence he will not necessarily lose the case.

Once a proper foundation for a defence has been laid by the defendant, the prosecution has the legal burden of disproving that defence.

Where the defendant raises a defence that goes beyond a denial of the prosecution case then he must lay a proper foundation for that defence.

2.2 DEFINITIONS

- The **legal** burden is the burden to prove or disprove a fact in issue;
- The **evidential** burden is merely a burden to produce evidence.

2.3 THE LEGAL BURDEN IN CRIMINAL CASES: GENERAL RULE

1. In criminal proceedings the prosecution bears the legal burden of proving every element of the offence charged, and disproving any defences raised, beyond reasonable doubt (*Woolmington v DPP* (1935)).
2. The legal burden never shifts except where presumptions operate.
3. Whether or not the legal burden has been discharged is decided at the conclusion of the evidence by the tribunal of fact (jury or bench of magistrates).

2.4 THE LEGAL BURDEN IN CRIMINAL CASES: EXCEPTIONS TO THE GENERAL RULE

A legal burden may be placed on an accused in relation to a specific defence raised. This is a new legal burden that arises by virtue of a defence and the accused must prove such a defence on a balance of probabilities.

1. **Common law:** Insanity under the M'Naughten rules.
2. **Express statutory exceptions** include:
   - s2 of the Homicide Act 1957: where diminished responsibility is raised as a defence to a charge of murder (*R v Dunbar* (1958));
   - s1(1) of the Prevention of Crime Act 1953: where the accused relies on a defence of lawful authority or

reasonable excuse in response to a charge of possession
of an offensive weapon;

- s2 of the Prevention of Corruption Act 1916: where a
gift is given or received by a public official, it will be
presumed that the gift was given or received corruptly
unless the contrary is proved by the accused;

- these exceptions are illustrative examples only: research
suggests that up to 40% of offences tried in Crown
Court impose a legal burden on the accused.

3. **Implied statutory exceptions** by virtue of s101 of the
Magistrates' Court Act 1981 which states: 'Where the
defendant … relies for his defence on any exception,
exemption, proviso, excuse or qualification, the burden of
proving that he falls within that exception, proviso, excuse
or qualification shall be on him.'

- The importance of s101 is that it places a legal burden
on the defendant where he relies upon a defence
provided by statute to a limited class of people, for
example, licence holders.

- The scope of the exception was widened by *R v Edwards*
(1975) where it was held that s101 of the *Magistrates'
Court Act* is merely 'declaratory of the English law' and
applies both to summary trials and trials on indictment.

- The House of Lords in *R v Hunt* (1987) offered
guidelines to courts charged with construing statutes in
accordance with s101:

  - it should not easily be inferred that Parliament
  intended to impose a legal burden on the accused;

  - courts should have regard to the intention of
  Parliament and the mischief at which the section is
  aimed;

  - courts should have regard to the ease or difficulty a
  party would have in discharging the legal burden;

  - the more serious the offence, the less likely that
  Parliament would have intended to impose a legal
  burden on the accused;

- where the statute is ambiguous, the accused should be given the benefit of the doubt.

2.5 THE EVIDENTIAL BURDEN IN CRIMINAL CASES

- Where a party has only an evidential burden on an issue, there is no obligation upon him to prove that issue; he is merely expected or required to adduce evidence.
- The nature of the evidential burden in a criminal case changes during the course of a trial.

Students should understand the nature of the evidential burden in the following situations:

1. Where the evidential burden is borne by the prosecution at the start of the trial (see section 2.5.1).
2. Where the evidential burden is borne by the accused at the close of the prosecution case (see section 2.5.2).
3. Where the evidential burden is borne by the accused by virtue of a defence which goes beyond a denial of the prosecution case (see section 2.5.3).
4. Where the evidential burden is borne by the accused by virtue of his reliance upon the defence of non-insane automatism (see section 2.5.4).

2.5.1 The evidential burden on the prosecution at the start of the trial

1. At the start of a trial, the prosecution has the evidential burden to produce evidence on every element of the offence charged.
2. In order to discharge this burden, the prosecution must produce sufficient evidence to justify a conviction if that evidence were to remain unchallenged. In other words, the prosecution must establish a *prima facie* case.

3. The court at the conclusion of the prosecution case will decide whether or not the evidential burden has been discharged. This process is sometimes referred to as 'passing the judge'.

2.5.2 The evidential burden on the accused at the close of the prosecution case

1. Once the prosecution has 'passed the judge' the evidential burden passes to the defence, but as it passes, the burden becomes less onerous.
2. If the prosecution fails to discharge its evidential burden, the accused will be entitled to be acquitted because the prosecution, by failing to produce evidence on every element of the offence charged, will be unable to discharge its legal burden of proof.
3. At the close of the prosecution case the accused is said to have an evidential burden because it is expected at that point in the trial that he will produce evidence in his defence. Failure to do so will not inevitably result in conviction.

2.5.3 The evidential burden where an accused raises a defence which goes beyond a denial of the prosecution case

A more onerous evidential burden falls on the accused where he relies on a defence which goes beyond a mere denial of the prosecution case. In that event, he must either produce evidence, or point to evidence already adduced by the prosecution, which raises the defence, or lays a proper foundation for the defence.

Examples of defences that go beyond a denial of the prosecution case:
* self-defence;

- duress;
- mechanical defect as the cause of an accident;
- reasonable excuse for failing to provide a breath test;
- provocation.

2.5.4 Evidential burden on accused where defence of non-insane automatism is relied upon

Because of the complex nature of this defence, the only way in which a proper foundation can be laid is by producing medical evidence in support. Failure to do so will result in the judge withdrawing the defence from consideration by the jury.

2.6 THE IMPACT OF THE HUMAN RIGHTS ACT 1998

1. s3(1) HRA 1998 requires judges and magistrates, so far as is possible, to construe legislation so as to give effect to the principles enshrined within the European Convention on Human Rights (ECHR).
2. Article 6(2) of the ECHR guarantees that any person charged with a criminal offence will be presumed innocent until the contrary is proved.
3. It is anticipated that the HRA 1998 may pose problems of construction for courts where legal burdens are imposed on defendants by statute, and particularly where such burdens are imposed, not expressly, but by implication under s101 of the Magistrates' Court Act 1980.

2.6.1 Decisions on article 6(2)

1. The European Court of Human Rights (ECtHR) in *Salabiaku v France* (1991) held that a reverse onus does not inevitably breach Article 6(2) but must be confined within

reasonable limits which take into account the importance of what is at stake and maintain the rights of the defence.

2. In *R v Lambert* (2001) the House of Lords dismissed an appeal based on violation of Article 6(2) because the Human Rights Act 1998 had not been enacted at the time of trial.

- The *Lambert* case involved s28 of the Misuse of Drugs Act 1971 which provides that an accused is entitled to be acquitted of possession of a controlled drug with intent to supply '(i) if he proves that he neither believed nor suspected nor had reason to suspect that the substance or product in question was a controlled drug…'.

- On a literal interpretation, s28 appears to impose a legal burden on the accused. A majority of the House was of the opinion, however, that s28 should be construed as imposing an evidential rather than a legal burden.

- Although this opinion was *obiter* since the appeal was dismissed, it suggests that courts might adopt a robust approach to construction of similar sections under the authority of s3(1) of the HRA 1998.

- Parliament will need to be explicit in imposing legal burdens, as was the case with the Terrorism Act 2000, otherwise courts are likely to follow the lead of the House of Lords by construing statutory provisions as imposing evidential burdens only.

2.7 THE LEGAL BURDEN IN CIVIL CASES

The legal burden in a civil case lies on the party who positively asserts the fact in issue and to whose claim or defence proof of that fact in issue is essential. In simple terms, **he who asserts must prove**.

1. Where it is not apparent from the papers which of the parties is making the positive assertion, the court may find that the legal burden lies with the party who would have least difficulty discharging that burden (*Soward v Leggatt* (1836); *Joseph Constantine Shipping v Imperial Smelting* (1942)).

2. Statute may decree which party bears the legal burden:
   - under s98 of the Employment Rights Act 1996, where an employee claims unfair dismissal he has the legal burden of proving only that he was dismissed; the legal burden lies with the employer to prove that the dismissal was fair;
   - under s171(7) of the Consumer Credit Act 1974, where a debtor claims that a credit bargain is extortionate the legal burden lies with the creditor to prove the contrary.

3. The legal burden may be fixed by agreement between the parties (*Chappell v National Car Parks* (1987)). Where the terms of the agreement are unclear, the courts will interpret the words of the agreement (*Hurst v Evans* (1917)).

2.8 THE EVIDENTIAL BURDEN IN CIVIL CASES

1. The claimant (who makes a positive assertion and bears the legal burden at the start of the trial) also has the evidential burden.

2. At the close of the claimant's case the evidential burden passes to the defendant.

3. At the end of the trial the court must decide whether the **legal** burden has been discharged.

2.9 THE STANDARD OF PROOF

1. There are two standards of proof, the criminal standard and the civil standard.

2. The standard of proof necessary to discharge the burden of proof relates to the legal, not the evidential burden.
3. The party who bears the legal burden on a particular issue will lose on that issue if the tribunal of fact considers the required standard of proof has not been reached.

2.9.1 The criminal standard of proof

1. Where the legal burden lies with the prosecution, the criminal standard of proof, beyond reasonable doubt, applies.
2. Where, exceptionally, the defendant bears a legal burden by raising a defence such as diminished responsibility or insanity, he need only discharge that legal burden to the civil standard, proof on a balance of probabilities (*R v Carr-Briant* (1943)).
3. Lord Denning, in *Miller v Minister of Pensions* (1947) explained both standards of proof. Of the criminal standard he said: 'If the evidence is so strong against a man as to leave only a remote possibility in his favour… the case is proved beyond reasonable doubt.'
4. Judges must be careful in directing juries as to the meaning of the term 'proof beyond reasonable doubt'. The prudent judge will adopt the wording in *R v Summers* (1952) that the jurors must be 'satisfied so that they feel sure' where they feel an explanation of the term is necessary.

2.9.2 The civil standard of proof

Lord Denning, in *Miller v Minister of Pensions* (1947), said of the civil standard: 'If the tribunal of fact thinks it **more probable than not,** the burden is discharged.' A 51% probability is sufficient to discharge the civil burden of proof. There are recognised exceptions to the general rule in civil cases where either the criminal standard or a standard higher than the normal civil standard of proof will be applied:

1. The standard of proof in committal proceedings for civil contempt of court is beyond reasonable doubt (*Dean v Dean* (1987)).

2. By virtue of a statutory requirement: for example under the Royal Warrant Act 1949, where an application is made for a war pension, the Minister must be satisfied beyond reasonable doubt that the claimant's application is not supported by the evidence (*Judd v Minister of Pensions and National Insurance* (1966)).

3. Where a serious allegation of crime is made in the context of civil proceedings, it has been suggested that a higher standard of proof is appropriate (*Thurtell v Beaumont* (1923)). *Hornal v Neuberger Products Ltd* (1957) is today regarded as more authoritative. That case suggests that the civil standard will always be the appropriate one, however serious the allegation.

4. It has been held that evidence capable of rebutting the presumption of the validity of a marriage must be 'strong, distinct and satisfactory' (*Piers v Piers* (1849)) or even 'evidence which satisfies beyond reasonable doubt' (*Mahadervan v Mahadervan* (1964)).

CHAPTER 3

COMPETENCE, COMPELLABILITY, SPECIAL MEASURES AND SILENCE

3.1 COMPETENCE: GENERAL RULE IN CRIMINAL CASES

1. A witness is competent if, as a matter of law, a court can receive his evidence.
2. He is compellable if, as a matter of law, his refusal to testify may give rise to contempt proceedings.
3. A witness who is competent will also be compellable unless he falls within an excepted category.

Statutory authority: s53(1) of the Youth Justice and Criminal Evidence Act 1999 (YJCEA 1999): 'At every stage in criminal proceedings all persons are (whatever their age) competent to give evidence.'

3.2 EXCEPTIONS TO THE GENERAL RULE IN CRIMINAL CASES

The accused:
- s1(1) CEA 1898
  s53(4) YJCEA 1999 –
  incompetent as prosecution
  witness unless ceased to
  be accused

EXCEPTIONS TO THE GENERAL RULE ON COMPETENCE AND COMPELLABILITY IN CRIMINAL PROCEEDINGS

The spouse of the accused:
- s53(1) and Sched. 4 YJCEA 1999;
- s80(3) PACE 1984

Vulnerable witnesses and children:
- Unsworn evidence – s55(2) YJCEA 1999;
- Special measures – s16 YJCEA 1999

3.2.1 Public policy exceptions to the general rule

1. **The Sovereign** is competent but not compellable.
2. **Diplomats** are competent, but compellability is dependent upon statutory rules (including the Diplomatic Privileges Act 1964).
3. **Bankers** are compellable where the bank is a party to the proceedings, but not otherwise (s6 Bankers' Books Evidence Act 1879).

4. **The accused** is a competent witness in his own defence but is not compellable:

> **Statutory authority**: s1 of the Criminal Evidence Act 1898: '(1) A person so charged shall not be called as a witness in pursuance of this Act except upon his own application.'

- The accused is incompetent as a witness for the prosecution (s53(4) YJCEA 1999) unless he is no longer liable to be convicted in the proceedings (s53(5)).

5. **The co-accused**: where there are two or more defendants charged on the same indictment, one accused ceases to be a co-accused and becomes competent as a prosecution witness where:
   (a) proceedings are discontinued by the prosecution;
   (b) he is acquitted;
   (c) the indictment is severed and separate trials are directed;
   (d) one accused pleads guilty.

6. **The accused's spouse** is competent and compellable for the defence unless jointly charged.
   (a) S/he is competent both for the prosecution (s53(1) of and Schedule 4 to the YJCEA 1999) and a spouse's co-accused
   (b) But is not generally compellable unless the spouse is charged with an offence listed in s80(3) of PACE 1984, namely:
      - the offence involves an assault on, or injury or threat of injury to, the wife or husband or a person who was at the material time under the age of 16; or
      - it is a sexual offence alleged to have been committed in respect of a person who was at the material time under
         (c) **Former spouses** are competent and compellable for all parties (s80(5) PACE 1984).

(d) **Failure of a spouse** to testify on behalf of a person charged shall not be the subject of comment by the prosecution (s80A PACE 1984).

3.2.2 Incompetence by virtue of personal characteristics

The presumption of competence under s53(1) of the YJCEA 1999 can be rebutted under s53(3):

'A person is not competent to give evidence in criminal proceedings if it appears to the court that he is not a person who is able to –
(a) understand the questions put to him as a witness; and
(b) give answers to them which can be understood.'

- This section has particular relevance for witnesses of tender years and for those suffering from mental incapacity (see *R v D (Video Testimony)* (2002)).
- Where the issue of competence arises, s54 YJCEA 1999 requires that the party seeking to call the witness must prove competence on a balance of probabilities.
- In deciding whether the witness is competent, the judge will consider the effect of any 'special measures' to which the witness might be entitled under s16 of the Act (see section 3.4 below).
- Any questioning of the witness to determine competence must take place in the presence of the parties, but in the absence of the jury and the court is entitled to assistance from expert witnesses where appropriate.

3.3 SWORN AND UNSWORN TESTIMONY

- A competent witness will give sworn testimony providing he is able to satisfy the requirements of s55(2) YJCEA 1999:

'The witness may not be sworn … unless –
(a) he has attained the age of 14, and
(b) he has sufficient appreciation of the solemnity of the occasion and of the particular responsibility to tell the truth which is involved in taking an oath.'

- Any competent witness who fails that test will be allowed to give unsworn testimony under s56 YJCEA 1999. As s55(2) makes clear, children under the age of 14 will automatically give their evidence unsworn, but the Act also allows adult witnesses to give unsworn testimony where they are unable to satisfy the test laid down by s55.

3.4 SPECIAL MEASURES DIRECTIONS

Eligibility:

Witness under 17: s16(1)(a)

Witnesses suffering from:

- Mental disorder – s16(2)(b)
- Impairment of intelligence or social functioning – s16(2)(a)(ii)
- Physical disability or disorder – s16(2)(b)

Non-child witness suffering from fear or distress – s17(1) and (4)

Reasons for Special Measures Directions to be given in open court:

Special Measures Directions under s16 YJCEA 1999

Judicial warning to jury to ensure direction does not prejudice accused – s.32

Nature of Special Measures

Screening – s23

Live link – s24

Evidence in private – s25

Removal of wigs and gowns – s26

Pre-recorded evidence in chief – s27

Pre-recorded cross-examination – s28

Aids to communication – s30

3.4.1 Eligibility for special measures

Witnesses who are *eligible for assistance* in the form of special measures directions fall into three categories:

1. Witnesses under the age of 17 who are automatically eligible (s16(1)(a));
2. Any witness the quality of whose evidence is likely to be diminished by reason of:
   - mental disorder (s16(2)(a)(i)); or
   - significant impairment of intelligence or social functioning (s16(2)(a)(ii));
   - a physical disability or disorder (s16(2)(b)).
3. Any non-child witness, the quality of whose evidence is likely to be diminished by reason of:
   - fear; or
   - distress

   in connection with testifying in the proceedings (s17(1)). In the case of an adult victim of a sexual offence, eligibility will be presumed unless the witness declines assistance (s17(4)).

3.4.2 Nature of special measures

The protections available for eligible witnesses are listed in ss 22–30 of the Act:

1. **Screening** (s23): an eligible witness may be prevented from seeing the accused, but not the judge, justices or jury or legal representatives.
2. **Live link** (s24(8)): 'a live television link or other arrangement whereby a witness, while absent from the courtroom or other place where the proceedings are being held, is able to see and hear a person there and to be seen and heard' [by the same persons as for screens].
3. Any witness under 17 will automatically be cross-examined by live link (s28).

4. **Evidence in private** (s25): persons of 'any description' other than:
    (i)   the accused;
    (ii) legal representatives;
    (iii) interpreters etc. assisting the witness;
    (iv) a single nominated and named representative of the press

    may be excluded from the courtroom whilst the eligible witness is testifying. This protection is available only where
    - the proceedings relate to a sexual offence; or
    - there are reasonable grounds for believing that some person other than the accused has sought or will seek to intimidate the witness while giving evidence (s25(4)).

5. **Removal of wigs and gowns** (s26).

6. **Evidence in chief by pre-recorded video** (s27): this is a very complex provision but, in outline, is as follows:

    (a) **Where the witness is under 17 at the time of hearing:**

    If the offence is sexual, or involves neglect, violence, kidnapping etc. (the full list of offences is set out in s21), the witness is deemed 'in need of special protection'. A video will take the place of live examination in chief unless:
    - facilities are not available; or
    - the court directs that all or part of the video should not be admitted in the interests of justice.

    Where the case is not sexual, so that the child is not in need of special protection, the child's evidence will normally be by video, but there is an additional ground for directing live examination in chief under s21(4)(c):
    - where the court is satisfied that compliance would not maximise the quality of the witness's evidence.

    (b) **Where the witness is over 17:**

    The court may make a direction for video-recorded evidence in chief unless it is of the opinion that it is not in the interests of justice (s27). Where that course

is taken the witness must be called to give evidence
under cross-examination at trial unless there is also

- a special measures direction for out-of-court cross-examination; or
- its admission is agreed.

7. **Video-recorded cross-examination and re-examination**
   (s28): this provision is entirely new and allows for
   mandatory cross-examination by video-recording for
   children under 17 who are 'in need of special protection'
   and discretionary video-taped cross-examination for
   children under 17 who are not in need of special protection
   and for other '*eligible*' adult witnesses.

8. **Aids to communication** (s30): an eligible witness may 'be
   provided with such device as the court considers
   appropriate with a view to enabling questions or answers to
   be communicated to or by the witness despite any disability
   or disorder or other impairment which the witness has or
   suffers from'.

3.4.3 General points on Special Measures Directions

1. Where the court makes a Special Measures Direction,
   s20(5) requires that reasons be given in open court. No
   application can be made to discharge a Special Measures
   Direction unless there has been a material change in
   circumstances.

2. Any evidence given by video recording under a Special
   Measures Direction will form an additional exception to
   the rule against hearsay.

3. On a trial on indictment, the judge must give such warning
   to the jury, under s32, 'as s/he considers necessary to ensure
   that the fact that the direction was given in relation to the
   witness does not prejudice the accused'.

3.5 COMPETENCE AND COMPELLABILITY IN CIVIL PROCEEDINGS: THE GENERAL RULE

1. In civil proceedings all adult witnesses are competent and compellable to give sworn evidence, including the claimant and the defendant.
2. Where one party challenges the competency of a witness, that issue will be determined at an early stage in the proceedings.

3.5.1 Exceptions to the general rule in civil proceedings

1. **Spouses**: under s1 of the Evidence Amendment Act 1853 a spouse is both competent and compellable in civil proceedings. It is doubtful whether the old case of *Monroe v Twistleton* (1802) remains good law, insofar as the case suggests that former spouses are incompetent in civil proceedings.
2. **Sovereigns and diplomats**: are competent but not compellable in civil proceedings.
3. **Bankers** are competent but not compellable unless the bank is a party to the action.
4. **Children**: in civil proceedings a person under the age of 18 is regarded as a child (s105 Children Act 1989).
   (a) A child may give sworn evidence provided s/he is able to satisfy the test laid down in *R v Hayes* (1977), namely that 'the child has sufficient appreciation of the solemnity of the occasion and the added responsibility to tell the truth, which is involved in taking an oath over and above the duty to tell the truth which is an ordinary duty of normal social conduct'.

(b) In civil proceedings, if a child is unable to satisfy the *Hayes* test, then, by virtue of s96 of the Children Act 1989, s/he may give unsworn evidence if, in the opinion of the court:

'(i) he understands that it is his duty to speak the truth; and

(ii) he has sufficient understanding to justify his evidence being heard.'

5. **Mentally ill or mentally handicapped** witnesses will be competent to give sworn evidence provided they can satisfy the *Hayes* test; where a mentally ill or mentally handicapped witness is unable to satisfy that test he will be incompetent in civil proceedings.

3.6 THE SILENCE PROVISIONS

1. By virtue of ss34–37 Criminal Justice and Public Order Act 1994, a jury is entitled to draw whatever inferences are proper from the failure of an accused to testify at trial, failure to mention when questioned or charged matters which are later relied on at trial, or failure to account for incriminating evidence.

2. As a result of the Criminal Procedure and Investigations Act 1997, adverse inferences can also be drawn from failure to comply with disclosure requirements. Disclosure requirements are dealt with in Chapter 14.

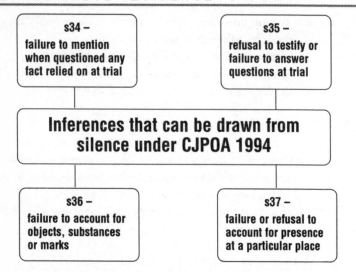

s34 –	s35 –
failure to mention when questioned any fact relied on at trial	refusal to testify or failure to answer questions at trial

Inferences that can be drawn from silence under CJPOA 1994

s36 –	s37 –
failure to account for objects, substances or marks	failure or refusal to account for presence at a particular place

A few important points relating to all four sections are:
- the sections do not make an accused person compellable in the technical sense of the term; under s35, failure to testify will not lay him open to contempt proceedings;
- a person cannot be convicted of an offence solely on the basis of an inference drawn from silence (s38(3)). The court or jury must be satisfied that the prosecution has established a *prima facie* case before inferences may be drawn.

3.6.1 s35 Criminal Justice and Public Order Act 1994

1. This section allows the court to draw such inferences as appear proper from the defendant's failure to give evidence or his refusal, without good cause, to answer any question at the trial (s35(3)).
2. The court must be satisfied that the accused is aware that the stage has been reached at which evidence can be given for the defence and that, if he chooses not to give evidence, inferences can be drawn (s35(2)).

3. The section does **not** apply where:
   (a) the accused's guilt is not in issue; or
   (b) it appears to the court that the physical or mental condition of the accused makes it undesirable for him to give evidence.

3.6.2 Judicial guidance on s35

1. Lord Taylor CJ, in *R v Cowan* (1996), advised that it would be open to courts to decline to draw adverse inferences, or to advise a jury against drawing such an inference from silence at trial only where there is 'some evidential basis for doing so or some exceptional factors in the case making that a fair course to take'.

2. The Judicial Studies Board has now published a total of six specimen directions based upon s35. The gist of the guidance is that judges must direct the jury that:
   - the accused is entitled to remain silent;
   - silence alone is not sufficient to justify a conviction;
   - the jury should consider any explanation for his silence and should draw inferences only where they conclude that silence must, sensibly, be attributed to the defendant having no answer.

3.6.3 s34 Criminal Justice and Public Order Act 1994

1. Similar inferences can be drawn under s34 where an accused fails to mention facts when questioned under caution or charged with an offence, which he later relies upon in his defence.

2. The substance of s34 is reflected in the words of the caution so the accused is effectively put on notice whenever the caution is administered:

> 'You do not have to say anything. But it may harm your defence if you do not mention when questioned something which you later rely on in court. Anything you do say may be given in evidence.'

3. Note that it is not only a refusal to answer questions when interviewed which may lead to inferences being drawn under s34; inferences can be drawn where the suspect **does** answer questions but fails to mention a fact which is relevant to the defence he eventually runs at trial.

4. Inferences may be drawn under s34 only where the suspect fails to mention 'a fact which in the circumstances existing at the time the accused could reasonably have been expected to mention when so questioned, charged or informed...'.

5. Section 58 YJCEA 1999 has amended ss34, 36 and 37 by inserting new ss34(2A), 36(4A) and 37(3A) which provide that the adverse inference provisions in ss34, 36 and 37 will not apply:
   - if the accused was not at an 'authorised place of detention' (a police station) at the time of his failure or refusal; and
   - if he was not allowed the opportunity of consulting a solicitor.

6. Where no specific defence is relied on at trial, the jury must be directed not to draw adverse inferences under s34 (*R v Moshaid* (1998)).

7. A defendant who chooses not to testify in his own defence must be wary of attempting to establish facts through the cross-examination of prosecution witnesses, since this could lay him open to inferences being drawn under s34.

8. Section 34 inferences may be drawn only where the defendant **relies** on facts he might reasonably have been expected to mention during interview. Questions that invite an accused to suggest an innocent explanation for prosecution evidence will not bring s34 inferences into

play. In those circumstances, he has not **relied** upon a defence; he has merely theorised at the invitation of prosecuting counsel (*R v Nickolson* (1999); *R v B (MT)* (2000)).

9. In deciding whether or not to draw adverse inferences under s34, the court is obliged to consider the 'circumstances existing at the time'. According to *R v Argent* (1997), this phrase encompasses the state of mind of the accused, his level of intelligence, command of English, and knowledge of the facts surrounding the offence.

3.6.4 Silence and human rights

1. The first case involving silence provisions to reach the ECtHR was *Murray v United Kingdom* (1996). On the facts of the case it was found that there was no breach of Article 6(1) or (2), but it was suggested there might well have been breaches had the accused been denied access to legal advice. The court stressed the importance of accurate and fair jury directions involving inferences from silence (this was not a problem in *Murray* since that trial took place before a Diplock court, where a judge sits without a jury).

2. In *Condron v United Kingdom* (2001) the ECtHR held that there had been a violation of Article 6(1): the right to a fair trial. It was emphasised that appeal courts must consider the fairness of trials, not just the safety of convictions, and *Condron* was distinguished from *Murray* on two grounds:
   - in *Condron* the defendants had given evidence at trial and explained why they had refused to answer questions at the police station (their solicitor formed the view that the appellants were suffering withdrawal symptoms and were unfit to be interviewed);
   - *Condron* was a jury trial and since juries are not required to give reasons for their verdicts, directions in the course of a judge's summing-up are vital.

CHAPTER 4

THE PROCESS OF TRIAL

Questioning of witnesses during the trial process is carried out in three stages: examination in chief, cross-examination and re-examination. Some rules of evidence are relevant purely at the examination in chief stage; others apply only in cross-examination.

Examination in chief

Refreshing the memory from documents:

- made or verified by witness;
- substantially contemporaneously;
- events fresh in memory.

Previous consistent statements inadmissible except:

- s26 Civil Evidence Act 1995;
- evidence of complaint in sexual case;
- *res gestae*/previous identification;
- statement in response to accusation.

Unfavourable and hostile witnesses:

- s3 Criminal Procedure Act 1865.

Cross-examination

Previous inconsistent statements:

- ss 4 and 5 Criminal Procedure Act 1865.

Cross-examination of police officers on conduct in other cases:

- *R v Edwards* (1991).

Finality rule on collateral questions:

- s3 Criminal Procedure Act 1865;
- bias;
- medical evidence of disability.

Rape cases:

- ss41–43 YJCEA 1999.

Re-examination

Previous consistent statement admissible in rebuttal.

4.1 EVIDENCE IN CHIEF

The purpose of examination in chief is for the party calling the witness to take the witness through his evidence and extract facts favourable to his case. No leading questions are permitted.

4.1.1 Refreshing the memory from documents

1. Any witness is entitled to refresh his memory from documents providing three conditions are satisfied:.

   (a) The document was **made by or verified** by the witness who wishes to refer to it (*R v Kelsey* (1981)) (see *R v Eleftheriou* (1993) for an illustration of how stringently this rule is enforced).

   (b) The note was made **substantially contemporaneously** with the events in question. *R v Fotheringham* (1975) suggests that a delay of 22 days in compiling the note is acceptable; in *R v Woodcock* (1963) it was held that a three-month delay is too long to be substantially contemporaneous.

   (c) At the time of compiling the note, the events must have been **fresh in the witness's memory**. In *R v Da Silva* (1990) guidance was given by Stuart-Smith LJ: 'Much will depend on the nature of the evidence to be given. Where, for example, a witness purports to give a verbatim account of a conversation, the note will need to have been made much nearer the time than if he merely purports to give the general effect of a conversation.'

2. A witness may therefore be allowed to consult a note not made sufficiently contemporaneously to satisfy the second condition, where he finds himself unable to remember an important point during the course of his testimony. In those circumstances the judge may allow him to refresh his memory on that single issue, after which the document should be removed from the witness.

3. Where a police officer refers to his notebook as an aide memoir, he can be cross-examined on other matters contained in the notebook that have not been referred to in examination in chief. The document then becomes an exhibit in the case.
4. Such an exhibit is relevant only to credibility in a criminal case; it cannot amount to corroboration of the witness's evidence, nor can it amount to evidence of any fact stated in it (*R v Virgo* (1978)).
5. There is no rule preventing witnesses from refreshing their memories before testifying from statements made at an earlier date (*R v Westwell* (1976)).

4.1.2 Refreshing the memory in civil proceedings

1. Witnesses can refer to documents created contemporaneously subject to the satisfaction of similar conditions as for criminal trials. The *Da Silva* principle extends to civil proceedings.
2. Hearsay statements can be admitted under s1 Civil Evidence Act 1995. Failure by a witness to satisfy the memory refreshing conditions will not prevent the admission of the document.
3. Where a document used to refresh memory becomes an exhibit, that document becomes evidence of any fact stated within it.

4.2 PREVIOUS CONSISTENT STATEMENTS (SELF-SERVING STATEMENTS)

General rule: Statements from the witness box to the effect that a similar account has been given on a previous occasion are inadmissible in both criminal and civil proceedings (*R v Roberts* (1942)). This is sometimes referred to as the rule against narrative.

4.2.1 Exceptions

1. **s6 Civil Evidence Act 1995**: in civil cases, with leave of the judge, a witness can refer in chief to a previous consistent statement. No leave is required where the purpose of adducing such evidence is to rebut a suggestion that the evidence has been fabricated.

2. Evidence of a complaint in a sexual case is admissible, but is relevant only to credibility and to negative consent. Guidelines were laid down in *R v Osborne* (1915):
    *   Evidence of a complaint is admissible in sexual cases providing **the complaint is both voluntary and speedy**.
    *   Rules apply equally to female and male complainants.
    *   Such a complaint is relevant both to credibility and to negative consent.
    *   The admission of the complaint is not limited to cases where the defence is consent, because one purpose for admitting the statement is to demonstrate the complainant's consistency.
    *   If the complainant does not testify, no other witness can give evidence of the complaint (*R v Wallwork* (1958)).

3. Previous consistent statements may be admissible as part of the *res gestae* (*R v Fowkes* (1856)).

4. **Previous identification**: Evidence that a positive identification has previously been made can be given either by the witness, or by a third party who witnessed the identification.

5. **Previous statements made in response to accusations**: Where an accused is challenged about incriminating acts and makes a statement exonerating himself that statement will normally be admissible, even though it is essentially self-serving. The justification for this exception is explained by Lord Widgery in *R v Storey* (1968):
    'A statement made voluntarily by an accused person to the police is evidence in the trial because of its vital relevance as

showing the reaction of the accused when first taxed with the incriminating facts ... the statement is not strictly evidence of the truth of what was said, but is evidence of the reaction of the accused which forms part of the general picture to be considered by the jury at the trial.'

4.3 UNFAVOURABLE AND HOSTILE WITNESSES

- An unfavourable witness is one who does not come up to proof yet acts in good faith.
- A hostile witness is one who does not wish to tell the truth.
- It is for the judge to decide whether a witness is unfavourable or hostile.

4.3.1 Dealing with unfavourable and hostile witnesses in criminal proceedings

1. Where a witness is merely unfavourable the party calling that witness can attempt to nullify the effect of his evidence through other evidence but cannot cross-examine the unfavourable witness.
2. Where the party calling a witness believes that witness to be hostile, then he may seek leave to treat the witness as hostile. If granted, the party who called the witness can:
   (a) contradict his evidence through other evidence; or
   (b) under s3 of the Criminal Procedure Act 1865, cross-examine the witness on his previous inconsistent statement.
3. In criminal proceedings the court cannot be invited to rely on the previous inconsistent statement of a hostile witness. The effect of treating a witness as hostile is to nullify the adverse effects of that witness's testimony.

4.3.2 Unfavourable and hostile witnesses in civil proceedings

1. In civil proceedings a previous inconsistent statement can be used either to discredit the witness's oral testimony, or as evidence in the case.
2. Even where a witness is merely unfavourable, leave may be sought to introduce a previous inconsistent statement under s6 Civil Evidence Act 1995.

4.4 CROSS-EXAMINATION

1. The purpose of cross-examination is to extract favourable facts from witnesses called by the other party and cast doubt on the opponent's case.
2. Questioning is not restricted to matters raised in chief and leading questions are permitted.
3. Any matters in dispute must be put to the witness, or it will be assumed that the facts, as stated by the witness, are true.
4. In a criminal trial involving several defendants, each has the right to cross-examine all witnesses.

4.5 PREVIOUS INCONSISTENT STATEMENTS

1. Any discrepancy between a previous statement and oral evidence can be put to witnesses in cross-examination (ss 4 and 5 Criminal Procedure Act 1865).
2. In criminal proceedings the inconsistency is relevant only to credibility although the Criminal Justice Bill 2000, if enacted without amendment, changes the position. Previous inconsistent statements will be admissible as evidence of the truth of their contents, as is the position in civil proceedings.

3. In civil proceedings (s6(1) Civil Evidence Act 1995) the judge can be asked to prefer the previous statement to the oral evidence.

4.6 CROSS-EXAMINING POLICE OFFICERS ON OTHER CASES

The Court of Appeal laid down guidelines in *R v Edwards* (1991) as to the circumstances in which police officers might be questioned about their conduct in other cases although the court declined to lay down hard and fast rules:

Guidelines:

(a) The acquittal of a defendant in Case A, where the prosecution case depended largely or entirely on the evidence of a police officer, does not normally render that officer liable to cross-examination as to credit in Case B.

(b) However, where Case A results in an acquittal in circumstances where a jury must have disbelieved a police officer's evidence relating to a disputed admission, then in Case B, where an admission is similarly disputed, it is proper that the jury should be made aware of the earlier case.

(c) However, where the acquittal in Case A does not 'necessarily' indicate that the jury disbelieved the officer, such cross-examination should not be allowed. A verdict of not guilty need not necessarily mean that the jury believed that a police officer had lied in evidence.

- It would seem that evidence that a previous jury verdict was **consistent** with perjury would not be sufficient.

- In *R v Guney* (1998) the Court of Appeal held that the defence is entitled to transcripts of decisions in which convictions have been quashed on the basis of the misconduct or lack of veracity of identified police officers. Transcripts should also be supplied where a trial judge discontinues a case for similar reasons.

4.7 COLLATERAL QUESTIONS

1. Collateral questions will normally, though not invariably, relate to the credit of the witness being cross-examined.
2. The general rule is that collateral questions may be asked, but the answer given by the witness must be treated as final.
3. Collateral questions were defined in *Attorney-General v Hitchcock* (1847): if a piece of evidence could have been introduced had the witness not given evidence, it is not collateral. If that evidence could not have been introduced in the absence of the witness, it is collateral.
4. An alternative test, which is easier to apply, is:

> Does the question relate solely to the witness rather than to a fact in issue? If the answer is 'yes', then the question is collateral.

The important question to be determined is whether the evidence relates to a fact in issue in the present trial.

Example
R v Burke (1858): an Irish witness gave evidence through an interpreter, having stated that he spoke no English. In cross-examination it was suggested he had spoken to two people in court in English. He denied that suggestion. That answer had to be treated as final since the witness's ability to speak English was not a fact in issue in the case. The question was admissible, but being collateral, was subject to the finality rule.

4.7.1 Exceptions to the finality rule

1. **Section 6 Criminal Procedure Act 1865**: all witnesses can be asked if they have any criminal convictions recorded against them (with the exception of the accused).
2. **Bias**: where an allegation of bias is made against a witness, a denial need not be treated as final (see *R v Mendy* (1976); *R v Phillips* (1936); *R v Busby* (1982)).
3. **Medical evidence of disability**: for example, an eye witness can be questioned about any eye condition which might affect the quality of his testimony. See *Toohey v Metropolitan Commissioner of Police* (1965) for a slightly unusual example.

4.8 RAPE CASES

Before ss41–43 YJCEA 1999 came into force, the relevant statutory provision governing cross-examination of complainants in rape cases was s2(1) of the Sexual Offences (Amendment) Act 1976.

- Section 2(1) was designed to offer protection for complainants, allowing cross-examination on previous sexual history only with leave.
- Section 2(2) limited leave to those circumstances where the judge believed that refusal to allow such cross-examination would be unfair to the accused.
- Case law following that Act resulted in leave being granted in almost every case where the accused relied upon consent by way of defence (see *R v Lawrence* (1977); *R v Viola* (1982); *R v Funderburk* (1990); *R v Redguard* (1991) and others by way of example).

Paul Boateng MP, giving evidence before the House of Commons Standing Committee which scrutinised the YJCEA 1999, identified the purpose behind ss41–43 of the

Act: 'The intention ... is to keep as much evidence of complainants' sexual behaviour out of trials as possible... Sexual history should be admitted only in very limited circumstances where it is really relevant to an issue at trial.'

4.8.1 s41 YJCEA 1999

1. Section 41(1) provides:
   'If at a trial a person is charged with a sexual offence, then, except with the leave of the court
   (a) no evidence may be adduced, and
   (b) no question may be asked in cross-examination by or on behalf of any accused at the trial, about any sexual behaviour of the complainant.'
2. Note that s41 deals with all *sexual offences* while s2(1) of Sexual Offences (Amendment) Act 1976 was restricted purely to rape cases.
3. 'Sexual behaviour' is defined in s42(1)(c) as:
   'any sexual behaviour or other sexual experience, whether or not involving any accused or other person, but excluding... anything alleged to have taken place as part of the event which is the subject matter of the charge against the accused.'
4. Thus cross-examination of the complainant about pre-offence behaviour towards the accused is allowed insofar as it forms part of the events leading up to the offence.
5. s41(4) states:
   'No evidence or question shall be regarded as relating to a relevant issue in the case if it appears to the court to be reasonable to assume that the purpose (or main purpose) for which it would be adduced or asked is to establish or elicit material for impugning the credibility of the complainant as a witness.'

4.8.2 The power to grant leave under s41(2)

1. Leave to cross-examine a complainant on previous sexual history may be granted in only four very limited circumstances:

   (a) **Where the issue is not one of consent** (s41(3)(a)). Cross-examination may be allowed where the defence is that the offence never took place, or, more worryingly, where the accused genuinely or mistakenly believed that the victim was consenting.

   • s42(1)(b) defines 'issue of consent' as:
   'any issue whether the complainant in fact consented to the conduct constituting the offence with which the accused is charged (and accordingly does not include any issue as to the belief of the accused that the complainant so consented)'.

   (b) **Where the behaviour occurred around the same time as the alleged offence** (s41(3)(b)):
   '[the sexual behaviour of the complainant] to which evidence or question relates is alleged to have taken place at or about the same time as the event which is the subject matter of the charge against the accused.'

   (c) **The 'Romeo and Juliet' scenario** (s41(3)(c)): This provision applies where the sexual behaviour is so similar to either:
   '[any] sexual behaviour of the complainant to which the evidence or question relates is alleged to have been, in any respect, so similar:

   (i) to any sexual behaviour of the complainant which (according to evidence adduced or to be adduced by or on behalf of the accused) took place as part of the event which is the subject matter of the charge against the accused, or

   (ii) to any sexual behaviour of the complainant which... took place at or about the same time as that event, that the similarity cannot reasonably be explained as a coincidence.'

- Under this limb, the sexual behaviour may take place over a wider time-frame than in s41(3)(b) but the behaviour must in some way or other be so striking that it is relevant to consent.
- This exception has been dubbed the 'Romeo and Juliet' scenario because the balcony scene provides a useful illustration. If the circumstances of an alleged rape involved the defendant climbing to a balcony and having intercourse with the complainant, his defence being that she had invited him to do so, evidence that she had similarly invited other men on previous occasions to climb to the balcony for the purposes of intercourse might well be admissible under this limb.

(d) **Evidence of sexual behaviour adduced by the prosecution** (s41(5))

This subsection permits leave

'(i) [where the evidence or question] relates to any evidence adduced by the prosecution about any sexual behaviour of the complainant; and

(ii) in the opinion of the court, would go no further than is necessary to enable the evidence adduced by the prosecution to be rebutted or explained by or on behalf of the accused.'

2. Even where one of those four exceptions above applies, leave may only be granted subject to the provisos below:

- 'A refusal of leave might have the result of rendering unsafe a conclusion of the jury or (as the case may be) the court on any relevant issue in the case' (s41(2)(b)).
- Leave may never be granted under the first three limbs if 'it appears to the court to be reasonable to assume that the purpose (or main purpose) ... is to establish or elicit material for impugning the credibility of the witness' (s41(4)).

- The evidence or questioning must relate only to specific instances of sexual behaviour (s41(6)). Thus, evidence of reputation can never be allowed in evidence.

3. Section 41(5) allows the defendant the opportunity to introduce evidence of previous sexual conduct to rebut an assertion made by the prosecution. Where, for example, the complainant was presented to the jury as a virgin at the time of the alleged rape, it would be open to the defence to introduce evidence in rebuttal of that assertion.

4.8.3 Early case law on ss41 and 42

The Human Rights Act 1998 (HRA 1998) threatens to undermine the protection afforded to complainants under s41 YJCEA. The case of *R v A (No. 2)* (2001), decided by the House of Lords, raised a number of important issues as the House struggled to construe ss41–43 in accordance with the requirements of Article 6 of the ECHR (the right to a fair trial).

1. Their Lordships held that a purposive approach to the construction of s41, as required under s3 HRA 1998, should be adopted. Admissibility was dependent upon relevance to the issue of consent, but trial judges must be satisfied before granting leave that excluding such evidence would breach the right to a fair trial.

2. Although the appeal related specifically to s41(3)(c), their Lordships provided useful guidance on s41(3)(a) and (b). Under s41(3)(a), which allows leave to cross-examine to be granted where evidence is relevant to an issue other than consent, Lord Hope identified a number of circumstances that might satisfy this paragraph. These included:
   (i) where the accused relies on a defence of honest belief in consent;
   (ii) where allegations of bias or fabrication are made against the complainant.

3. Under s41(3)(b), which allows leave to be granted where evidence relates to sexual behaviour 'at or about the same time' as the alleged rape, Lord Steyn suggested that evidence relating to an invitation to have sex earlier on the same evening would satisfy the provision; and Lord Hope suggested that the phrase might properly be interpreted as encompassing conduct which occurred several minutes to several hours before the alleged rape. He thought it unlikely that an incident occurring several days before could be construed as 'at or about the same time'.

4. On s41(3)(c) Lord Hope concluded that the test was not satisfied on the facts as there was no similarity with the complainant's sexual behaviour on a previous occasion. s41 was designed to prevent cross-examination on the basis that because the complainant had had consensual intercourse on a previous occasion she was more likely to have consented on this occasion. The onus, in those circumstances, is upon the defendant to demonstrate that the similarity in the complainant's behaviour cannot be explained on the grounds of coincidence.

4.9 PROCEDURAL POINTS

1. Applications for leave are heard in private in the absence of the complainant (s43(1)).

2. The court must state reasons for granting or refusing leave in open court in the absence of any jury and specify the extent of the leave granted (s43(2)).

3. Applications for leave should normally be made within 28 days of committal and should be accompanied by 'a summary of the evidence it is proposed to adduce and of the questions it is proposed to put'.

4.10 RE-EXAMINATION

1. The purpose of re-examination is for the party calling the witness to restore the credibility of that witness and emphasise points favourable to his case.

2. Questions in re-examination are normally restricted to matters raised in cross-examination.

3. Whilst evidence of a previous consistent statement is inadmissible in chief, it may be allowed in re-examination to rebut an assertion made in the course of cross-examination. Where, for example, it is suggested to a witness in cross-examination that his evidence is a recent fabrication, that allegation can be rebutted by introducing evidence in re-examination relating to a previous consistent statement.

4. No new evidence can be introduced once the jury has retired (*R v Gearing* (1966)).

CHAPTER 5

THE NEED FOR SUPPORTING EVIDENCE

Corroboration or judicial warnings

Judicial warning to take care required

Disputed identification evidence (*R v Turnbull* (1977))

Corroboration required by statute:

s89(2) RTA 1984;

s13 Perjury Act 1911;

s1 Treason Act 1795

Judicial direction required

Lies told by accused (*R v Lucas* (1981));

Alibi defence raised by accused (*R v Burge, Hurst and Pegg* (1996))

Discretionary warning to take care

Evidential basis for believing witness's evidence might be 'suspect'

5.1 GENERAL RULE

1. 'Corroboration' is generally unnecessary in England and Wales. A court can act on the unsupported testimony of one witness or one document, even where other evidence contradicts that evidence.

2. At common law, very complex rules had evolved requiring corroboration of certain categories of evidence before that evidence could be acted upon; other evidence required a warning to the jury to take care before relying upon uncorroborated evidence.

3. As a result of the Criminal Justice and Public Order Act 1994 (CJPOA 1994), the requirement for corroboration in its legal sense has almost been eradicated. Despite that Act a limited number of exceptions remain; hence it is still necessary to understand the nature of corroboration.

5.1.2 The limited requirement for corroboration today

1. s32(1) CJPOA 1994 states that:
   'Any requirement whereby at a trial on indictment it is obligatory for the court to give the jury a warning about convicting the accused on the uncorroborated evidence of a person merely because that person is
   (a) an alleged accomplice of the accused, or
   (b) where the offence charged is a sexual offence, the person in respect of whom it is alleged to have been committed,
   is hereby abrogated.'
2. As a result of s32(1), corroboration in its strict legal sense is relevant today only in those circumstances (detailed in section 5.2.1) where there can be no conviction in the absence of corroboration.

5.2 LEGAL DEFINITION OF 'CORROBORATION'

1. The legal definition was laid down by Lord Reid CJ in *R v Baskerville* (1916):
   'Evidence in corroboration must be independent testimony which affects the Accused by connecting him or tending to connect him with the crime. In other words it must be evidence which implicates him, that is which confirms in some material particular not only that the crime has been committed, but also that the prisoner committed it.'

2. It must therefore:
   (i) be admissible in itself;
   (ii) derive from a source independent of the witness whose evidence needs corroborating; and
   (iii) show not only that the crime was committed, but that it was committed by the accused.

5.2.1 Statutory corroboration required

Corroboration is required by statute in three situations:

1. **Exceeding the speed limit**: s89(2) Road Traffic Act 1984: 'A defendant cannot be convicted of exceeding a speed limit on the opinion evidence of one witness.'
   If the police rely on an instrument, such as a speed gun or speedometer reading, a single police officer can give evidence, as it is a matter of fact (not opinion) that the machine registered a particular speed (*Brighty v Pearson* (1938)).

2. **Perjury**: s13 Perjury Act 1911: 'A person shall not be liable to be convicted of any offence against this Act, or of any offence declared by any other Act to be perjury or subornation of perjury, or to be punishable as perjury or subornation of perjury solely upon the evidence of one witness as to the falsity of any statement alleged to be false.'

3. **Treason**: s1 Treason Act 1795 provides that a person cannot be convicted of high treason, which involves the death or kidnap of the Queen or her heirs, without the oaths of two credible witnesses. The Criminal Law Revision Committee recommended the repeal of this statutory requirement as long ago as 1972.

5.3 SUSPECT WITNESSES: DISCRETIONARY WARNINGS

1. By virtue of s32(1) CJPO Act 1994 a judge has a discretion, not a duty, to warn the jury to take care before

relying upon the evidence of any witness where he is satisfied that there is an evidential basis for so doing.

2. Lord Taylor CJ laid down guidelines relating to the circumstances in which discretionary warnings should be given in *R v Makanjuola* (1995):

   (a) Whether or not a warning is given, and the nature of such a warning, are matters of judicial discretion in all cases. A warning may, but need not be given in respect of accomplices testifying for the prosecution and complainants in sexual cases, as is the position with any other witness. It will depend on the circumstances of the case, the issues raised and the quality of the witness's evidence.

   (b) A warning to take care before relying on a witness's evidence should not be given merely because a witness is a complainant in a sexual case or an accomplice. There must be some other aspect of the evidence, such as lying, previous false complaint, or bias before such a warning is given.

   (c) Warnings should be given as the judge reviews the evidence in the course of his summing up rather than as a separate legal direction.

   (d) Although the substance of each warning is discretionary, judges should avoid repeating the old and technical corroboration warning.

   (e) The Court of Appeal will be slow to interfere with the exercise of a judge's discretion unless that exercise is unreasonable in the *Wednesbury* sense.

3. There is no requirement on a judge to direct the jury as to which evidence is and is not capable of amounting to corroboration in the technical *Baskerville* sense.

4. According to *R v B (MT)* (2000) he should nevertheless identify to the jury any 'independent supporting evidence'. Such evidence might be found in lies told by the accused either in court or pre-trial (see section 5.4 below), the silence of the accused (s34–37 CJPOA 1994 (see section

3.6)), or admissions made by the accused during the course of testimony that support the prosecution case.

5.4 LIES TOLD BY THE ACCUSED

1. Lies told by a defendant may be probative of guilt and may support other evidence.

2. Wherever the prosecution proposes to rely upon the lies of a defendant, a *Lucas* direction should be given to the jury. The judge must direct the jury that a lie may be probative of guilt only where each of four conditions, laid down in *R v Lucas* (1981) are satisfied:
   (a) the lie must be deliberate;
   (b) it must relate to a material issue;
   (c) the motive must be a realisation of guilt and fear of the truth;
   (d) It must be clearly shown to be a lie by admission or independent evidence.

3. A modern version of the test, which expands its application to alibi defences, was laid down in *R v Burge, Hurst and Pegg* (1996). A direction is normally required where:
   - the defence raises an alibi;
   - the judge considers it desirable or necessary to suggest that the jury should look for support of a piece of evidence (e.g. disputed identification evidence), and draws attention specifically to lies told or allegedly told by the accused;
   - the prosecution suggests that something said in or out of court was a lie, and relies on that lie as evidence of guilt;
   - although the prosecution does not seek to rely on a lie as evidence of guilt, the judge believes there is a danger that the jury might do so.

4. The direction should include two points:
   (i) the jury must be satisfied that the lie is either admitted or proved beyond reasonable doubt; and

(ii) they must be reminded that the mere fact the accused lied is not itself evidence of guilt since the accused might lie for innocent reasons; only if the jury is convinced that the lie was told for no innocent reason could such a lie support the prosecution case.

5.5 IDENTIFICATION EVIDENCE

Identification evidence has long been regarded as potentially unreliable. In 1976, following a number of notorious miscarriages, a Committee, chaired by Lord Devlin, considered necessary reform. Their recommendations were given effect in *R v Turnbull* (1977) and by Codes of Practice issued under the Police and Criminal Evidence Act 1984.

5.5.1 Safeguards at a pre-trial stage

Police officers should consider which method of identification is most appropriate in each case. Four procedures are regarded as acceptable, depending on the circumstances:
(i)   identification parade;
(ii) group identification;
(iii) video identification;
(iv) confrontation.

1. Traditionally, the four alternatives were ranked in terms of reliability in the order above, with the identification parade the preferred option and the confrontation the least favoured. Under Code D of the new Codes of Practice issued in April 2002, video identification is elevated from third position to rank alongside the identification parade as the preferred procedure. As a result, there is likely to be an increase in the number of video identifications held.

2. Whatever form of identification procedure is selected, police officers must record a description from the witness

before the procedure takes place. This description must be disclosed to the defence before trial.

3. Identification evidence, like any other evidence upon which the prosecution proposes to rely at trial, is subject to exclusion under s78 Police and Criminal Evidence Act 1984 where the court believes its inclusion would adversely affect the fairness of the proceedings. That may be the position where major breaches of Code D have occurred.

5.5.1.1 Identification parades

1. Annex A of Code D governs the conduct of an identification parade. Briefly, some of the important paragraphs require:

   (a) the officer conducting the parade should not be involved in the case;

   (b) the suspect must be told of his right to have a solicitor present;

   (c) the parade must be photographed or videoed, and everything said and done should take place in the presence and hearing of the accused or his representative;

   (d) where no representative is present, the parade must be videoed; in any event the procedure must be video-recorded or a colour photograph taken;

   (e) at least eight 'stooges' must take part and they should resemble the suspect as far as possible;

   (f) witnesses should be brought into the room where the parade takes place individually and there should be no opportunity for witnesses to communicate with each other.

2. *R v Forbes* (2001) clarified the circumstances in which an identification parade must be held. It was stressed that the provisions of Code D are mandatory, and additional unwritten conditions are not to be inserted. Where a suspect disputes a witness's identification and consents to a parade, then a parade must be held. There is nothing in the

words of the Code to justify a distinction as to quality of identification evidence between that of a police officer and a member of the public.

3. Where a witness claims he would be unable to identify an offender, there is no requirement to hold an identification parade, despite a request from the suspect (*R v Nickolson* (1999)).

4. Where a witness provides a description of an offender but does not identify him, there is no need to hold an identification procedure (*R v Oscar* (1991)).

5.5.1.2 Video identification

1. Annex B of Code D regulates this procedure, which is quite similar to the identification parade.

2. It must include eight 'stooges' who, so far as possible, resemble the accused. The suspect and his lawyer should be given an opportunity to view the film and should be allowed to be present when the video is shown to the witnesses. If this does not occur, then the procedure must be recorded on video.

3. As with the identification parade, there must be no opportunity for witnesses to communicate with each other.

5.5.1.3 Group identification

1. This involves a witness viewing the suspect amongst an informal group of people.

2. The procedure may take place with the consent and co-operation of a suspect or covertly where a suspect refuses to co-operate with other procedures, or where the officer in charge of the investigation believes this form of identification is more satisfactory than an identification parade or video identification.

3. Annex E of Code D requires that a colour photograph be taken of the scene immediately after the identification is made.

5.5.1.4 Confrontation

1. When no other method of identification is available, confrontation may be used.
2. This will normally take place in a police station, with the witness being asked 'Is this the person?'.
3. It is, for good reason, regarded as the least reliable form of identification.

5.6 SAFEGUARDS AT TRIAL

Guidelines, which apply in every criminal case involving disputed identification evidence, were established in *R v Turnbull* (1977). These are:

1. The judge must issue a **warning** to the jury to take care before relying upon identification evidence. This should take place in any case involving disputed identification evidence and should include an explanation of the reasons why caution is necessary.
2. The judge should direct the jury to look closely at the **circumstances** in which the identification took place: the lighting, distance, time for observation etc.
3. The judge should point out to the jury any **weaknesses** in the identification evidence. Were there, for example, any discrepancies between the description initially supplied by the witness and the appearance of the defendant?
4. The judge must consider the **quality** of the identification evidence: if the quality is good, then the case can be left for the jury to consider providing that a *Turnbull* warning is given; if the evidence is poor then the judge must withdraw the case from the jury unless there is supporting evidence.
5. The judge should identify any evidence that **supports** the reliability of the identification evidence.

5.6.1 The nature of supporting evidence

- Lord Widgery suggested that a failure by the accused to testify at trial, or a refusal to answer questions at the police station, could not amount to supporting evidence. This situation has now changed as a result of ss34–37 Criminal Justice and Public Order Act 1994 (see section 3.6). Silence can provide support for disputed identification evidence, as can lies told by the accused and false alibis, subject to the required *Lucas* direction.

● Supporting evidence is that which tends to support or confirm other evidence. It need not amount to corroboration under the old *Baskerville* test. Judges should identify to jurors evidence that is capable of providing support; whether or not such evidence does provide support is a matter for the jury to decide.

5.6.2 The circumstances in which a Turnbull warning must be given

1. Case law suggests that the safest course is to deal with all cases of disputed identification evidence in accordance with the *Turnbull* guidelines. Failure to apply the guidelines is likely to result in convictions being quashed on appeal (see *Reid v The Queen* (1990)).

2. There is no special wording for formulating *Turnbull* directions, providing that the sense and spirit of the guidelines is complied with (*Mills v R* (1995)).

3. Although recognition evidence is regarded as less dangerous than identification of a stranger, a *Turnbull* warning remains necessary (*R v Bentley* (1991)).

4. *R v Thornton* (1994) suggests that where the accused admits his presence at the scene, but denies participation in the events that led to the charge, a full *Turnbull* warning is required.

5. In *R v Slater* (1995) *Thornton* was distinguished: where presence at the scene is admitted, and the distinctive appearance of the accused eradicates the danger of an eye-witness mistakenly identifying the wrong person, no *Turnbull* warning is necessary.

CHAPTER 6

CHARACTER AND CONVICTIONS

6.1 INTRODUCTION

The general rule is that evidence of a defendant's bad character is inadmissible in criminal proceedings, though subject to exceptions; in civil proceedings, the bad character of a party to the proceedings is admissible where relevant to a fact in issue.

The following diagram illustrates the fundamental rule and the exceptions to that rule in criminal cases.

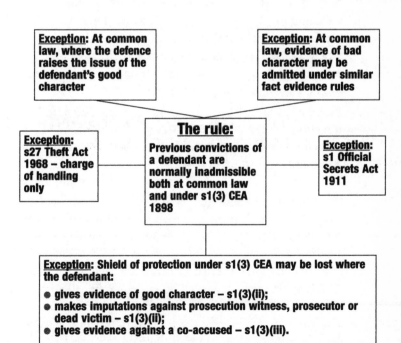

Exception: At common law, where the defence raises the issue of the defendant's good character

Exception: At common law, evidence of bad character may be admitted under similar fact evidence rules

Exception: s27 Theft Act 1968 – charge of handling only

The rule:
Previous convictions of a defendant are normally inadmissible both at common law and under s1(3) CEA 1898

Exception: s1 Official Secrets Act 1911

Exception: Shield of protection under s1(3) CEA may be lost where the defendant:

- gives evidence of good character – s1(3)(ii);
- makes imputations against prosecution witness, prosecutor or dead victim – s1(3)(ii);
- gives evidence against a co-accused – s1(3)(iii).

6.2 CHARACTER AND CONVICTIONS IN CIVIL PROCEEDINGS

1. Evidence of character is admissible if it **amounts to a fact in issue**, for example evidence of a person's reputation in an action in defamation.
2. Under s11 Civil Evidence Act 1968 the previous convictions of a party to an action are admissible if they are **relevant to the facts in issue**, for example a conviction for reckless driving may be relevant to a civil action in negligence arising out of the same incident. The party seeking to admit a criminal conviction must indicate his intention in his statement of case.
3. Any witness who gives evidence in civil proceedings, including the claimant and defendant, can be cross-examined on his credibility as a witness (s6 Criminal Procedure Act 1865), although, where such cross-examination is regarded as collateral, the witness's answers will be treated as final (see section 4.7).

6.3 CONVICTIONS OF PERSONS OTHER THAN THE ACCUSED IN CRIMINAL CASES

1. s6 Criminal Procedure Act 1865: witnesses can always be cross-examined on previous convictions. Where the conviction is denied, it can be proved by a certificate of conviction.
2. s74(1) Police and Criminal Evidence Act 1984 states that: 'In any proceedings the fact that a person other than the accused has been convicted of an offence… shall be admissible in evidence for the purpose of proving, where to do so is relevant to any issue in those proceedings that that person committed that offence.'

(a) The Court of Appeal has advised that s74 should be used sparingly and is subject to the court's discretion to exclude under s78.

(b) The prosecutor should make it plain precisely how the conviction is relevant to an issue in the case and the judge must direct the jury carefully, explaining the relevance of the conviction. (See *R v Kempster* (1989) and *R v Manzur and Mahmoud* (1997) for restrictions on the use of s74.)

6.4 CONVICTIONS OF THE ACCUSED IN CRIMINAL CASES: STATUTORY RULES

General rule: At common law, the prosecution cannot introduce evidence of the bad character of the accused. Where a witness inadvertently mentions his previous convictions, the judge has a discretion to discharge the jury.

Exceptions

(a) **Section 1(3) Criminal Evidence Act 1898**: an accused cannot be asked questions about bad character or convictions unless he falls within subsections s1(3)(i), (ii) or (iii). These exceptions will be dealt with fully at 6.7.

(b) **Section 27 Theft Act 1968**: where an accused is charged with handling stolen goods, the prosecution can introduce evidence that he has handled or disposed of stolen goods from a theft during the 12 months prior to the present offence or that he has been convicted of theft or handling within five years of the present offence. This section is used sparingly by prosecutors and evidence is commonly excluded by judges under s78(1) PACE 1984.

(c) **s1 Official Secrets Act 1911** allows the prosecution to introduce evidence of the character and convictions of the accused.

6.5 COMMON LAW EXCEPTIONS: ADMISSION OF EVIDENCE OF BAD CHARACTER

Bad character evidence is most commonly admitted under ss1(3)(i), (ii) and (iii) which allow for the cross-examination of an accused in certain circumstances. An accused can only be cross-examined where he chooses to testify. Where an accused does not testify, the following common law rules are applicable.

- The prosecutor can introduce evidence of character and convictions if this is admissible as similar fact evidence. (Similar fact evidence is dealt with in Chapter 7.)
- Where the defence raises the issue of the accused's good character, the prosecution may be allowed to provide the jury with the full picture. In *R v Winfield* (1939) the accused, who was charged with indecent assault, did not give evidence himself, but called a character witness to tell the jury that he was always a 'perfect gentleman' in the company of women. The prosecutor was allowed to produce evidence of previous convictions relating to dishonesty.

6.6 EVIDENCE OF GOOD CHARACTER IN CRIMINAL CASES

1. Where an accused has good character and testifies on his own behalf, the judge is obliged to direct the jury upon the relevance of his good character. The leading case is *R v Vye* (1993) and consequently the good character direction is known as a *Vye* direction.

2. According to *Vye*, good character is relevant both to:
   - the defendant's credibility as a witness; and
   - the issue of guilt,

   and the jury must be so directed.

3. A direction as to the relevance of good character to credibility need be given only where the accused testifies in his own defence; where an accused of good character chooses not to testify, he remains entitled to a direction on the relevance of his good character to the issue of guilt.

4. In a trial involving two defendants, one of good character, the other of bad character, the judge may choose either to say nothing about the bad character of the second defendant, or to direct the jury that they have heard nothing about his character and must not speculate. There is no discretion to make no mention of the first defendant's good character.

5. Judges are entitled to modify the terms of the *Vye* direction in the light of the special circumstances of a case. Lord Steyn gave useful guidance on this in *R v Aziz* (1995).

6.7 THE CRIMINAL EVIDENCE ACT 1898

s1(3) Criminal Evidence Act 1898 (as amended by s67 YJCEA 1999) provides the accused with a shield of protection, by preventing him from being cross-examined on previous convictions; it goes on to create exceptions under which that shield can be lost. The accused will lose his shield where:

'(i) the proof that he has committed or been convicted of such other offence is admissible evidence to show that he is guilty of an offence with which he is then charged; or

(ii) he has personally or by his advocate asked questions of the witnesses for the prosecution with a view to establish his own good character, or has given evidence of his good character, or the nature or conduct of the defence is such as to involve imputations on the character of the prosecutor or the witnesses for the prosecution or the deceased victim of the alleged crime; or

(iii) he has given evidence against any other person charged in the same proceedings.'

6.7.1 Interpretation of s1(3)

In *Jones v DPP* (1962) the majority in the Court of Appeal held that the words 'tending to show' in s1(3) should be interpreted as meaning 'reveal to the jury for the first time'. Since the appellant had told the jury of his own volition that he had been in trouble with the police on a previous occasion, there was no reason to disallow cross-examination on that statement. A similar decision was reached in *R v Anderson* (1988).

6.7.2 Preliminary points on s1(3)

The shield of protection provided by s1(3) that prevents cross-examination on previous criminal convictions can be thrown away by the accused if he brings himself within any of the three exceptions, ss1(3)(i) (ii) or (iii). Before focussing on the detail of those exceptions, it is useful to list some preliminary points:

1. Where cross-examination is allowed, it is relevant only to credibility. It has no relevance to guilt or innocence.

2. Whether subsections (i) or (ii) have been brought into play is a matter for judicial discretion (or judgement) and counsel should seek leave before cross-examining on character.

3. Although judges rarely exercise discretion in favour of defendants who fall foul of the three subsections, the discretion remains. Factors which may persuade a judge to

exercise discretion by disallowing cross-examination on convictions are:

(a) a weak prosecution case;

(b) an overwhelming prosecution case;

(c) where imputations made against a prosecution witness are minor;

(d) where the criminal record of the accused is particularly bad.

4. Where cross-examination is allowed, it remains subject to the common law rules of relevance (in *Maxwell v DPP* (1935) it was held that cross-examination on a previous acquittal is irrelevant and inadmissible).

5. *R v Butterwasser* (1948) is authority for the proposition that an accused will not lose his shield under the Act if he does not give evidence.

6.7.3 Cross-examination on character under s1(3)(i)

1. This is both the most difficult exception to understand, and the least important.

2. The prosecutor can cross-examine on character where the proof an accused has committed or been convicted of some other offence is admissible as evidence in chief against him. If, for example, character evidence is admissible under similar fact evidence rules (see Chapter 7) the accused can be cross-examined on that evidence, providing:

    ● the evidence is admissible in its own right; and

    ● it tends to show the accused is guilty of the present offence.

3. s1(3)(i) also allows cross-examination on previous convictions where these can be proved as part of the facts in issue, for example where the charge is driving whilst disqualified.

6.7.4 Cross-examination on character under s1(3)(ii)

There are two limbs to this subsection, i.e. two ways in which the shield can be lost:

1. **Where evidence is given by the accused or his counsel to establish good character.**

   This is similar to the common-law rule, but subsection (ii) must be used wherever the accused testifies on his own behalf.

   - An accused will not lose his shield where a defence witness, without invitation, speaks of his good character (*R v Baker* (1912)).

   - He may lose his shield without making any direct claim of good character. In *R v Samuel* [1956] the accused, charged with theft, merely claimed to have returned lost property on previous occasions, but was held to have fallen foul of the subsection.

   - Wearing a regimental blazer while testifying was held in *R v Hamilton* (1979) to be insufficient to bring him within s1(3)(ii).

   - *R v Marsh* (1994) illustrates the potential breadth of the subsection: the accused, a professional rugby player who was charged with inflicting grievous bodily harm on an opponent in the course of a match, quite accurately claimed to have no criminal convictions. The judge ruled that such an assertion would lay him open to cross-examination on his poor disciplinary record involving violence on the field of play.

2. **Where imputations are made against a prosecution witness, prosecutor or the deceased victim of alleged crime.**

   An accused may lose his shield under s1(3)(ii) by making imputations against a prosecution witness, the prosecutor or the deceased victim of the alleged crime.

- This part of the subsection is potentially very wide, allowing for cross-examination where an accused suggests that a prosecution witness is biased, or where he denies making a confession in circumstances that suggest that a prosecution witness might have lied.
- *Selvey v DPP* (1970) established that even where an imputation is an integral part of a defence, the subsection will be invoked.
- Until the mid-1980s a line of authorities suggested that judges retained a discretion to exclude cross-examination under s1(3)(ii) where prejudice might result. However, in *R v Burke* (1986), the Court of Appeal decided that those authorities were wrong insofar as they ignored *Selvey*. Even where the previous convictions are similar to the offence charged and will inevitably result in prejudice, the shield will be lost, and discretion will rarely be exercised (though see *R v Davison-Jenkins* (1997) for an alternative view).
- The one partial exception to the *Selvey* principle arises where an accused is charged with rape: suggesting that a complainant consented to intercourse will not result in loss of the shield (*R v Turner* (1944)).
- There is often a fine line between a robust denial of a charge and an imputation against a prosecution witness (see *R v Tanner* (1978); *R v Nelson* (1978); *R v Britzman and Hall* (1983)).
- It should be noted that a defendant can freely attack the character of anyone not called as a prosecution witness (with the exception of the deceased victim) without losing his shield of protection.

6.7.4.1 Recent guidelines on the operation of s1(3)(ii)

The Court of Appeal laid down its most recent set of guidelines on the operation of s1(3)(ii) in *R v McLeod* (1994):

1. The purpose of cross-examination on bad character relates to credibility, not to disposition to commit the sort of offence charged. However, the mere fact that the offences are similar and might incidentally suggest a disposition to commit the sort of offence charged does not make such cross-examination improper.

2. Prolonged or extensive cross-examination on previous offences should be avoided.

3. Similar defences that have been rejected by juries on previous occasions may be legitimate matters for cross-examination since they are clearly relevant to credibility.

4. Where objection is taken to cross-examination that goes beyond the bare facts of previous convictions, the matter must be raised at the time the objection arises. The Court of Appeal will be unwilling to question the exercise of a judge's discretion on such a matter where no objection is made.

5. Where a prosecutor cross-examines on previous convictions, the judge must direct the jury that such cross-examination is relevant only to credit and they should not consider that it shows disposition or propensity to commit the offence they are considering.

6.7.5 Cross-examination on character under s1(3)(iii)

1. In a trial involving more than one accused, in which D1 gives evidence against D2, D2 is entitled to cross-examine D1 on bad character **as of right**. The prosecutor can also rely on this subsection, but, unlike the co-accused, must first seek leave of the judge. The trial judge has discretion as to whether or not to allow cross-examination by the prosecution.

2. It is for the court to determine whether or not one accused has given evidence against another by applying the either/or test laid down in *Murdoch v Taylor* (1965):

(a) Has the accused given evidence supporting the prosecution case against his co-accused? OR

(b) Has the accused undermined the defence of his co-accused?

3. Where either or both of those conditions is satisfied, the co-accused has a right to cross-examine on previous convictions. This is, of course, a common occurrence in cases involving multiple defendants, with each running what are popularly known as 'cut-throat' defences.

4. An example of the subsection in operation is found in *R v Davis* (1975). Two accused were charged with theft of a gold chain in circumstances where the property must have been taken by one of them. Davis was careful in chief not to lay the blame on his co-accused, but in the course of cross-examination admitted that his co-accused must have taken the chain since he, Davis, had not. That was sufficient to bring s1(3)(iii) into play. Mere inconsistency between defences, on the other hand, is insufficient, as in *R v Bruce* (1975) and *R v Crawford* (1998).

5. *R v Varley* (1982) illustrates the difficulties that subsection (iii) can pose for defendants. Varley and his co-accused were jointly charged with robbery. The co-accused admitted taking part but claimed he acted under duress, threats to his life having been made by Varley. Varley denied taking part and claimed the defence of duress was a pack of lies. There was no dispute that the co-accused, in alleging duress, fell within s1(3)(iii); it was held on appeal that Varley had undermined the defence of his co-accused by denying there was any duress.

6. Where an accused falls foul of s1(3)(iii), there is no discretion to restrict cross-examination, which must be allowed to its fullest extent, subject only to the requirement of relevance (*R v Reid* (1989)).

6.7.6 Statutory restrictions on cross-examination under s1(3)

1. Under s16(2) Children and Young Persons Act 1963 where an accused is over the age of 21, no cross-examination under s1(3) CEA 1898 will be allowed in relation to offences committed whilst under the age of 14.

2. Under s4(l) of the Rehabilitation of Offenders Act 1974 no reference may be made to convictions which are 'spent'. Although s7(2) of the same Act expressly excludes criminal proceedings, a Practice Direction issued by Lord Widgery CJ in 1975 recommended:
   'Both court and counsel should give effect to the general intention of Parliament by never referring to a spent conviction when such reference can be reasonably avoided …
   … no-one should refer in open court to a spent conviction without the authority of the judge, which authority should not be given unless the interests of justice so require.'

   - Talbot J in *R v Nye* (1982) explained the circumstances in which cross-examination might be allowed on spent convictions: 'the jury must not be misled and no lie must be told to them…'. He emphasised that any discretion should be exercised, so far as is possible, favourably towards the accused.

6.8 PROPOSALS FOR REFORM

The Criminal Justice Bill 2002, published in November 2002, makes radical proposals for reforms to the present law governing the admission of bad character evidence in criminal proceedings. The reforms are dealt with in outline only since they are unlikely to be enacted in the very near future and because amendments may well be made during the passage of this Bill.

1. Clause 81 defines 'bad character evidence' as including evidence that shows a person has committed an offence, or behaved or is disposed to behave in a way that might be viewed with disapproval by a reasonable person.

2. Clauses 81–92 of Chapter 1 in Part II of the Act propose a statutory scheme regulating its admissibility. Evidence of a defendant's bad character will be admissible where:
   (a) all parties agree to its admission;
   (b) the defendant introduces the evidence himself;
   (c) bad character evidence amounts to 'important explanatory evidence'. (This phrase is clarified in cl 83(2) which states that evidence is only admissible under this heading if without it, the court would find it impossible or difficult to understand other evidence.)
   (d) the evidence is relevant to an important issue between prosecution and defence;
   (e) it has significant probative value in relation to an important issue;
   (f) it corrects a false impression given by the defendant about himself;
   (g) the defendant has attacked the character of another person.

3. Evidence of previous acquittals may be admissible in circumstances such as those approved by the House of Lords in *R v Z* (2000) (see section 7.6 below).

4. Evidence which shows the defendant's propensity to commit offences or to be untruthful will become admissible.

5. Evidence that is relevant to issues between the defendant and a co-accused will be admissible at the behest of the co-accused.

6. The admission of bad character evidence will be subject to a discretion to exclude in the interests of fairness which will replicate the test under s78 PACE 1984.

CHAPTER 7

SIMILAR FACT EVIDENCE

DEALING WITH PROBLEM QUESTIONS ON SIMILAR FACT EVIDENCE IN CRIMINAL CASES

Step 1
Consider the test in *Makin v Attorney-General for New South Wales*:
● Can the prosecution demonstrate a purpose for admitting SFE that goes beyond establishing propensity?
If the answer is **NO**, SFE should be excluded.
If the answer is **YES**:

Step 2
Identify the purpose for admitting the SFE.

If the purpose is to **establish identity**, and where SFE is the sole or main evidence by which identity is to be established, **apply the test in *DPP v Boardman*:**

Is there a **striking similarity** between the SFE and the facts in issue that cannot be explained on the grounds of coincidence?

If there is a purpose for admitting SFE beyond establishing identity, or where there is other evidence to establish identity, **apply the test in *DPP v P*:**

Is there a sufficient relationship or **sufficient probative force** to justify its admission despite its prejudicial effect?

Step 3
If the answer is **NO**, SFE should be excluded.
If the answer is **YES**, SFE should be admitted.

7.1 General rule

The general rule, which applies to all bad character evidence, was considered in Chapter 6: evidence that a person charged with a criminal offence has been guilty of misconduct on previous occasions is generally inadmissible. The rationale for the exclusionary rule is twofold:
(i) such evidence is irrelevant; and
(ii) it is highly prejudicial to the accused.

7.2 Exceptions to the general rule

It is useful, for revision purposes, to be aware of all the exceptions to the general rule, although most of these exceptions are dealt with elsewhere in this book.

1. Past convictions as pre-conditions of liability (for example, where a person is charged with driving while disqualified, it is necessary to introduce evidence to prove the disqualification) (sections 6.2 and 6.7.3).

2. Similar fact evidence (which forms the subject matter of this chapter).

3. *Res gestae* (section 9.3).

4. Statutory exceptions, e.g. s27(3) Theft Act 1968 (section 6.4).

5. Rebutting claims of good character at common law (section 6.5).

6. Exceptions to s1(3) Criminal Evidence Act 1898 (section 6.7).

7. Cross-examination on previous misconduct where the court is already aware of misconduct, for example *R v Anderson* (1988); *Jones v DPP* (1962) (section 6.7.1).

7.3 Introduction

1. The admission of SFE is exceptional. It will be admitted only where it is relevant to an issue in the case and has a

degree of probative force that outweighs its prejudicial effect. Mere evidence of bad character or dishonesty is not enough, even where the previous offences are similar in nature to the conduct charged. The evidence must show, not just that the accused is the sort of person who might have committed this sort of offence, but that he actually committed it.

2. When admitted, similar fact evidence goes to the issue of guilt, not just credibility. This is an important distinction: character and convictions admitted under s1(3) Criminal Evidence Act 1898 are relevant only to credibility.

3. Similar fact evidence may be used either by the prosecution or the defence.

4. The prosecution will most commonly seek to admit SFE as part of their case; exceptionally, they may apply to admit SFE at a later stage by way of rebuttal evidence.

5. Where a defendant is charged with similar offences against two or more 'victims', the admission of SFE takes on a new significance. The judge will have to decide whether the offences committed against each complainant are sufficiently similar to be admissible under SFE rules. If so, then the evidence of both complainants will be admissible in relation to each charge; if not, the jury must either be directed to consider each offence separately, or the judge must sever the indictment and direct that the two offences be dealt with at separate trials.

7.3.1 Case example

In *R v Kidd* (1995) the appellant was convicted of going equipped for theft, having been found lying face down with a metal detector in a field which formed part of an archaeological site. He claimed he had been drinking and was walking with the detector to a friend's house with a view to selling the detector. Evidence was admitted of previous convictions for theft from archaeological sites committed with the help of a metal detector. It was held that the essential feature, following *DPP v P* (1992), is 'whether the probative force in support of an allegation that an accused person committed a crime is sufficiently great to make it just to admit the evidence.' The appellant's similar convictions were highly relevant to rebut his defence and were properly admitted. The judge directed the jury that the mere fact the appellant had committed similar offences previously did not necessarily mean he was guilty on this occasion.

7.4 THE DEVELOPMENT OF SFE

While *DPP v P* is the leading case on SFE today, the earlier case of *Makin v A-G for NSW* (1894) remains of importance.

7.4.1 Makin v Attorney-general for NSW (1894)

1. This was the first case to lay down rules on SFE. A husband and wife were charged with murdering a baby in their care. During the investigation, police discovered the remains of 13 other babies in the gardens of three houses previously occupied by the Makins. There was no evidence to show how any of these babies had died, but the inference that arose because of the sheer number of dead infants was that the Makins must have murdered all 14.

2. Lord Herschell in the Privy Council formulated two rules:

   (a) An exclusionary rule, known as the 'forbidden chain of reasoning'. Under this rule, evidence which shows merely that the accused has a propensity to commit certain crimes is inadmissible (*Noor Mohamed v R* (1949)).

   (b) The mere fact that the evidence adduced tends to show the commission of other crimes does not make it inadmissible if it is relevant to an issue before the jury.

It may well be relevant in deciding if the acts of the defendant were designed or accidental or to rebut a defence.

3. The co-existence of these two rules means that there is a thin dividing line between admissible SFE and evidence that is forbidden under the first rule. (See, for example, *R v Straffen* (1952) and *R v Ball* (1911).)

4. In cases involving allegations of a sexual nature, the courts created new principles in order to get around the prohibition on propensity evidence (*Thompson v R* (1918)).

7.4.2 *DPP v Boardman* (1975)

1. The House of Lords sought in this case to clarify the rules laid down in *Makin*.

2. From a combination of the opinions of the House in this case it is possible to formulate a fairly precise test for admitting SFE. The two important rules are:

   (a) **Relevance**: this is a matter of law for the judge to decide.

   (b) **Probative force**: does the probative force of the evidence outweigh its prejudicial effect? This is a matter for judicial discretion or judgement.

3. Each of these rules will be satisfied by a single test:

> Evidence as to the similar facts and as to the main fact in issue must display such a close or **striking similarity**, or such an underlying unity, that if accepted, would in common sense be inexplicable on the grounds of coincidence.

4. Other principles that can be identified from the opinions of the Law Lords are:

(a) The same rules for establishing admissibility apply to all cases. There is no special rule for cases involving sexual misconduct.

(b) The admissibility of SFE does not depend upon any particular defence other than a general denial. However, the nature of the defence or possible defence is one of the factors that the judge should take into account when considering whether the probative force of SFE outweighs its prejudicial effect.

7.5 SIMILAR FACT EVIDENCE TODAY: *DPP v P* (1992)

1. In *DPP v P*, the defendant was convicted of rape and incest against two daughters under the age of 13. He appealed on the ground that the trial judge was wrong to have tried the counts relating to each daughter together.

2. Lord Mackay, in the leading judgment in the House of Lords, ruled that striking similarity is not necessary in every case, before allowing the evidence of one complainant to support the testimony of another.

3. Lord Mackay formulated the following test:
'whether there is material upon which the jury would be entitled to conclude that the evidence of one victim, about what occurred to that victim, is so related to the evidence given by another victim, about what happened to that other victim, that the evidence of the first victim provides strong enough support for the evidence of the second victim to make it just to admit it notwithstanding the prejudicial effect of admitting the evidence.'

4. The test, then, involves examining the relationship between each piece of evidence and considering the degree of support that one piece provides for the other. If the probative value of the evidence is sufficiently high to justify its admission despite its prejudicial effect, then the evidence should be admitted.

7.5.1 Where identity is in issue

1. Lord Mackay seemed to suggest in *DPP v P* that in cases where the identity of the offender is in issue, something akin to striking similarity would be required to support the identification.

2. The preferred view today is that striking similarity is necessary only where the uniqueness of the circumstances forms the sole or main basis of the prosecution's case. Where other evidence supports evidence of identity, there is no need to establish striking similarities (*R v W (John)* (1998)).

3. Prior to 1998 the Court of Appeal had approved two approaches:
    (i) The **'sequential'** approach where the jury first decides whether there is striking similarity between the previous misconduct and the alleged facts of the case. If so, they go on to consider whether the defendant committed Offence A. If he did, they are entitled to conclude that the defendant also committed Offence B (*R v McGranaghan* (1995)).
    (ii) The **'pooling'** or **'cumulative'** approach which applies only where the various allegations of misconduct form the basis of separate charges in the indictment. The first question for the jury using this approach is whether the same person committed all the offences. If so, they may add together the various pieces of evidence relevant to the issue of identity in order to decide whether the offender was the defendant (*R v Downey* (1995)).

4. In *R v W (John)* the House of Lords favoured the second approach.

7.5.2 Collusion

Where the defence alleges that SFE should not be admitted because of the danger that witnesses have colluded together and concocted their evidence, the preferred approach of the courts today is that in *R v H* (1995):

- The House of Lords decided that collusion does not, in general, affect the admissibility of evidence; it affects its weight.
- The issue of collusion is therefore best left to the jury, not to the judge, to consider.
- In such cases the judge should assume that the evidence is true in determining admissibility, but should direct the jury that they must satisfy themselves that the similar fact evidence is free from collusion before they can rely on it to support the prosecution case.

7.6 SIMILAR FACT EVIDENCE BASED ON A PREVIOUS ACQUITTAL

1. In *Sambasivam v Public Prosecutor, Federation of Malaya* (1950) it was held by the Privy Council that the principle of double jeopardy was not limited to preventing a second prosecution for the same offence, but also prevented the Crown, in a subsequent prosecution, from adducing evidence to show that a defendant was actually guilty of a charge of which he had previously been acquitted.

2. This principle was regarded as entrenched until the recent House of Lords decision in *R v Z* (2001) which has effectively overruled the *Sambasivam* principle.

3. The House of Lords ruled that the admissibility of such evidence would be subject to the judge's discretion to exclude it after weighing its prejudicial effect against its probative force; and further, would remain subject to the

overriding discretion to exclude evidence in the interests of fairness under s78 PACE 1984.

7.7 USE OF SIMILAR FACT EVIDENCE BY THE DEFENCE

1. There is no restriction on an accused producing evidence of a co-accused's general disposition in an endeavour to prove that he was less likely than his co-accused to have committed the offence, provided that such evidence is relevant.

2. Relevance is the sole criterion for admitting SFE as part of the defence case: there is no need to show that the probative value of such evidence outweighs its prejudicial effect.

   Case examples

   (a) In *Lowery v R* (1984) two defendants were jointly charged with the sadistic killing of a girl. The evidence suggested that either one or both of the accused had committed the murder. Lowery's co-accused was allowed to call a psychologist who testified that Lowery was more likely to have committed the offence than his co-accused because of his aggressive personality. The trial judge's decision to admit that evidence was upheld by the Privy Council.

   (b) *R v Neale* (1977) provides a useful contrast. Two defendants were jointly charged with arson and manslaughter. Defendant 1 raised an alibi defence, but sought to admit evidence that Defendant 2 had started fires on a number of occasions in the past. That evidence was inadmissible because it had no relevance to the defence of Defendant 1.

3. There is no restriction upon the defendant producing evidence which simply points away from himself (*R v Apps* (1998)).

4. The case of *R v Lobhan* (1995) emphasises that there is no discretion to exclude relevant defence evidence (s78 PACE 1984 covers only prosecution evidence).

7.8 SIMILAR FACT EVIDENCE IN CIVIL CASES

1. A much more relaxed approach to the admission of SFE is adopted in civil proceedings, with circumstantial evidence of misconduct on a previous occasion being commonly admitted as logically probative of a fact in issue (*Mood Publishing Co. Ltd v de Wolfe Publishing Ltd* (1976)).
2. SFE will be admitted if it is logically probative and provided it is neither oppressive nor unfair to the other party.
3. The other side must have fair notice of SFE.

7.9 PROPOSALS FOR REFORM

1. The Law Commission in its Report No. 273 criticised the tests in *Boardman* and *DPP v* P as vague and over-reliant upon judicial discretion.
2. The Criminal Justice Bill 2002 proposes abolition of the present rules relating to SFE under cl 82. Instead, the admission of all evidence of bad character will be governed by the new statutory regulations.
3. Evidence of the defendant's conviction for an offence of the same description as the one with which he is charged will generally be admissible. Such evidence must not be admitted where, upon application by the defendant to exclude the evidence, 'it appears to the court that the admission of the evidence would have such an adverse effect on the fairness of the proceedings that the court ought not to admit it'.
4. Evidence of propensity to commit offences of the kind with which a defendant is charged will be admissible except where propensity makes it no more likely that he has committed the present offence.

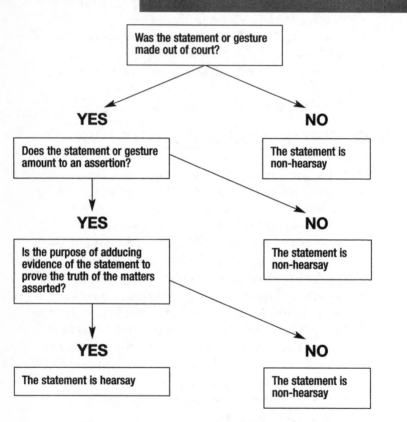

Was the statement or gesture made out of court?

YES   **NO**

Does the statement or gesture amount to an assertion?

The statement is non-hearsay

YES   **NO**

Is the purpose of adducing evidence of the statement to prove the truth of the matters asserted?

The statement is non-hearsay

YES   **NO**

The statement is hearsay

The statement is non-hearsay

8.1 HEARSAY EVIDENCE: A RULE OF EXCLUSION

The rule: An out of court statement is inadmissible as evidence of any fact or opinion contained in it. A statement made otherwise than in the course of giving evidence in court is inadmissible for the purpose of proving the truth of the words it contains; if tendered for any other relevant purpose, for example the mere making of the statement, then it is original evidence.

1. Although the rule is accurately stated above, it is difficult to follow and even more difficult to apply. A much easier definition of hearsay is the following:

   Hearsay is:
   (a) anything said or written outside the courtroom **if**
   (b) it is being used to prove the truth of what is contained in those words or writing.

2. Deciding whether a particular statement is hearsay or not involves turning the above statements into two questions:
   (a) **Was the statement made out of court?** If the answer is yes, go on to the second question. If the answer is no, the statement is non-hearsay.
   (b) **What is the purpose of the witness repeating/ producing the statement in court?** If the purpose is to suggest that the words spoken or written were true, then the statement is hearsay; if there is any other reason for repeating/producing the statement in court, then the statement is non-hearsay.

Example 1

D is charged with murdering V, an act witnessed by W. W could plainly give original evidence of what he saw. Suppose W tells a third party, X, that he saw D murder V, before he, W suffers a complete mental breakdown. Can X attend court and tell the jury what W told him he had seen?

Applying the two questions:

(1) The statement from W to X was made out of court.

(2) The purpose of repeating W's statement in court is to suggest that the words used were true and that D did indeed murder V. That statement is hearsay.

Example 2

Suppose that D is in fact innocent. Instead of D being charged with murder, D brings an action in defamation against W. Would X be allowed to testify as to what D told him?

Applying the two questions:

(1) The statement from W to X was made out of court.

(2) The purpose of X repeating W's statement in this scenario is not to prove that the W's words were true, simply to prove the words were spoken. In that event, the words are non-hearsay.

---

3. The exclusionary rule is applied stringently in criminal cases (see *R v McLean* (1967)).

4. The standard textbook definition of hearsay derives from *Subramaniam v Public Prosecutor* (1956). Subramaniam (S) was charged with unlawful possession of ammunition under emergency regulations. It was a defence to the charge to have lawful excuse for the possession, and S sought to testify that he had been captured by terrorists and acted under duress. The trial judge ruled he could not state in evidence what the terrorists said to him. The Privy Council held that such evidence was admissible since the object of such evidence was not to establish the truth of what the terrorists said to him, but merely the fact that the statement was made and the effect of the threat upon the defendant.

8.2 SCOPE OF THE HEARSAY RULE

1. The hearsay rule applies equally to statements made orally (*R v Teper* (1952)), in writing (*R v Lydon* (1986)) or by means of gestures (*R v Gibson* (1887)).

2. While the rule is justified on the grounds that hearsay evidence is potentially unreliable, and because of the impossibility of cross-examining on hearsay evidence, the

cases of *Sparks v R* (1964) and *R v Turner* (1975) illustrate that the rule can disadvantage defendants as well as prosecutors.

3. The House of Lords in *R v Kearley* (1992) recognised a further form of hearsay evidence: **the implied assertion**. The House of Lords by a 3:2 majority found that evidence of what was said by several different people, both on the telephone and in person, indicating that they wished to purchase drugs, was hearsay and inadmissible. The purpose of repeating the words used by the callers was not to prove merely that the words were spoken, but to show that the callers believed Kearley was involved in the supply of drugs and were correct in that assumption. On that basis the words were hearsay.

4. Proposals for reform of the hearsay rule are dealt with at section 11.8.

8.3 AVOIDANCE OF THE HEARSAY RULE

1. Judges have, from time to time, sought to restrict the scope of the hearsay rule for reasons of practicality.

2. In *R v Chapman* (1969), it was held that where a witness testifies that a doctor, in accordance with s2(2)(b) Road Safety Act 1967, indicated there was no medical objection to conducting a breath test, such a statement is not hearsay. The statement was construed (clearly wrongly) as non-hearsay in order to ensure that doctors are not routinely called to testify in routine cases.

3. Where police officers viewed a video recording from the security camera in a shop and identified a person seen to be stealing goods, the officers were able to give original, rather than hearsay evidence of what occurred in the shop when the video recording was inadvertently erased (*Taylor v Chief Constable of Cheshire* (1987)).

4. There is no breach of the hearsay rule where a police officer gives evidence to the effect that an eye-witness, who has no clear recollection, positively identified the accused at an identification parade (*R v Osbourne; R v Virtue* (1973)).

5. Neither sketches made by police officers at the direction of an eye-witness (*R v Percy Smith* (1976)) nor photographs (*R v Cook* (1987)) are regarded as hearsay.

8.4 EXCEPTIONS TO THE HEARSAY RULE IN CIVIL CASES: THE CIVIL EVIDENCE ACT 1995

1. One of the principal reasons for the development of the hearsay rule was because of the involvement of lay persons, particularly lay jurors in the trial process.

2. One of the principal reasons for the decline of the rule in civil proceedings is because of the decline in the involvement of lay persons.

3. Judges, it is felt, are capable of appreciating that evidence varies in terms of quality and reliability. Evidence which lacks reliability will be accorded less weight by professional judges.

4. The Civil Evidence Acts 1968 and 1972 were important steps towards admitting hearsay statements in civil proceedings more liberally, but the Acts were unnecessarily complex and many believed they did not go far enough.

5. The Civil Evidence Act 1995 (CEA 1995) repealed Part I of the 1968 Act and simplified the rules considerably; the new Act was based upon the principle that hearsay evidence should be admissible in civil proceedings, but subject to certain safeguards.

6. Procedural matters are dealt with by the Civil Procedure Rules (CPR) rule 33.

8.4.1 The substance of the Civil Evidence Act 1995

1. Section 1(1) of the CEA 1995 states that 'In civil proceedings evidence shall not be excluded on the ground that it is hearsay'. The effect of this is to make all hearsay statements admissible in civil proceedings.
2. Section 1(2)(a) adopts the standard common law definition of hearsay.
3. Section 1(2)(b) makes clear that all hearsay evidence is admissible whether it is first-hand, second-hand or has passed through multiple hands.
4. A 'statement' is defined in s13 as 'any representation of fact or opinion however made'. The term includes written statements, oral statements and gestures and, under the Civil Evidence Act 1972, statements of opinion.
5. Where a party seeks to introduce evidence that is admissible in its own right, the CEA 1995 will not apply (s1(3) and (4)). An example of evidence admissible in its own right would be a statement admitted under ss3–6 Criminal Procedure Act 1865 which is used to discredit a hostile witness. Because such a statement is admissible without recourse to the CEA 1995, the safeguards, including the Notice Procedure, imposed by s2 CEA 1995 do not apply.

8.4.2 Safeguards under the CEA 1995

Section 2 CEA 1995 lays down safeguards that are designed to counter the potential unreliability of hearsay evidence.
1. Subsection (1) deals with the requirement upon the party adducing the hearsay evidence to notify other parties of the intention to do so and to provide details of that evidence. This ensures that other parties in the proceedings are not taken by surprise, and gives them the opportunity, if it is practicable, to insist upon the attendance of a witness.

2. Time limits for the serving of notice are laid down by CPR rule 33.4. Failure to serve notice in accordance with rule 33.4 does not affect the admissibility of the statement but will affect the weight accorded to the statement (s2(4) CEA 1995).

3. The notice procedure can be waived by agreement between the parties (s2(3)).

4. Where hearsay evidence is adduced at trial, it is open to other parties under s5(2) CEA 1995 to attack the credibility of the hearsay witness by demonstrating that the witness has made another contradictory statement. This can be done by producing any evidence which would have been admissible had the hearsay witness testified in person.

5. Section 5(2) is designed to counter the disadvantage of being unable to cross-examine on a hearsay statement and to enable the judge to form a view about the weight that can properly be accorded to the hearsay statement.

6. Where a party wishes to make use of s5(2) that party must serve notice of his intention upon the party proposing to adduce the hearsay statement.

8.4.3 Weight attaching to hearsay statements under the CEA 1995

1. Section 2(4) CEA 1995 places responsibility for assessing the quality of hearsay evidence with the trial judge.

2. In deciding how much weight to accord to hearsay statements, the judge is obliged to consider all those circumstances that might affect the reliability of the evidence.

3. Listed in s4(2) of the Act are guidelines to assist judges rather than hard and fast rules.

4. An overview of the factors which judges should consider makes it clear that hearsay evidence continues to be regarded with some scepticism.

5. Section 4(2)(a) advises judges to consider the reasons why a party has chosen to adduce hearsay evidence in preference to calling the witness. If there is no valid reason for relying upon hearsay evidence instead of calling the witness, then little weight will be given to that evidence.

8.4.4 Supplementary matters

1. Section 6 deals with previous statements of witnesses. The CEA 1995 does not merely apply to the statements of witnesses who are not called to give evidence in person; it applies equally to a previous statement made by a person who gives oral testimony where that witness has also made a written or oral statement previously.
2. Subsection (2) goes on to say that a party who intends to call a person as a witness may not adduce evidence of a previous statement except with leave of the court or for the purpose of rebutting a suggestion that his evidence has been fabricated.
3. Section 7 deals with common law exceptions to the hearsay rule. A number of common law exceptions were expressly preserved by s9 Civil Evidence Act 1968. Where a statement is admissible under a common law exception to the rule against hearsay there is no need for the party seeking to adduce the statement to follow the procedures and safeguards contained in ss2–6 CEA 1995 with the exception of informal admissions. These become subject to the above procedures relating to safeguards and reliability.

8.4.5 Overview of the Civil Evidence Act 1995

1. In civil proceedings, evidence shall not be excluded on the ground that it is hearsay.
2. Unless the parties agree otherwise, a party proposing to adduce hearsay evidence in civil proceedings must serve notice on the other party/ies and, on request, such

particulars as are reasonable and practicable in order to allow him to deal with any matters arising from the hearsay evidence.

3. In assessing the weight to be given to hearsay evidence in civil proceedings, the court shall have regard to any circumstances from which inferences can reasonably be drawn as to the reliability or otherwise of the evidence.

4. The Civil Evidence Act 1995 does not abolish the common law exceptions to the hearsay rule, though it does supersede the exception covering informal admissions.

CHAPTER 9

COMMON LAW EXCEPTIONS TO THE HEARSAY RULE

Was witness dead victim of homicide? Try dying decalarations.

Was statement spontaneous and event shocking? (Witness need not be deceased victim). Try *res gestae*.

COMMON LAW EXCEPTIONS

Was statement:
(a) against interest
(b) in course of duty
(c) as to public or general rights
(d) as to pedigree?
All admissible at common law.

If hearsay statement is inadmissible at common law, consider ss23 and 24 CJA 1988 if documentary hearsay (Chapter 10); if statement could be a confession, consider admissibility under s76(2) PACE 1984.

9.1 INTRODUCTION

There are three common law exceptions to the hearsay rule:
(a) statements of persons since deceased;
(b) *res gestae* statements;
(c) statements in public documents.

9.2 STATEMENTS OF PERSONS SINCE DECEASED

Witnesses are entitled to adduce in evidence the oral statements of persons who have died before trial in circumstances where a court is able to assume that such a statement is reliable. Such statements are admissible as evidence of the truth of their contents. At common law, five situations are recognised:

- dying declarations;
- declarations against interest;
- declarations in the course of duty;
- declarations as to public or general rights;
- declarations as to pedigree.

9.2.1 Dying declarations

1. Dying declarations by the victim as to the cause of his injuries are admissible at a trial for murder or manslaughter provided:
   (a) at the time the statement was made the victim was under a **settled, hopeless expectation of death**; and
   (b) at the time the statement was made the witness would have been a competent witness if called to give evidence.

2. A dying declaration can either identify the assailant, or exonerate someone.

3. The justification for admitting dying declarations is that it is assumed that death-bed statements, made in full knowledge of impending death, are likely to be reliable.

4. The victim need not die immediately after making the statement, providing at the time it was made, he expected to die (*R v Bernadotti* (1869)).

5. *R v Jenkins* [1869] illustrates how stringently the courts will examine the pre-conditions for admissibility of dying

declarations: an officious clerk, coming upon a seriously injured young woman, asked her for an account of how she had been injured and wrote out her statement. Being legally well informed, he added to the statement that the victim had no hope of recovery, read the statement to her and asked her if she agreed with the words. She changed the final words to 'I have no *immediate* hope of recovery'. That was fatal: there was no longer a settled, hopeless expectation of death (note the mnemonic for this test spells SHED!).

9.2.2 Declarations against interest

The sort of statement admissible under this heading would include an admission that a debt is owed or that property is held as trustee rather than owner (*R v Rogers* (1995)).

9.2.3 Declarations in the course of duty

Declarations in the course of duty of a person since deceased are admissible whether the statement is oral or in writing. This exception applies where a person has made a report or kept a record because he was under a duty to do so (see *The Henry Coxon* [1878]). Such a record must have been made:

1. roughly contemporaneously with the activity referred to;
2. the duty must have been legal or professional rather than moral; and
3. there must have been no obvious motive on the part of the maker of the statement to misrepresent or distort the facts.

9.2.4 Declarations as to public or general rights

1. A statement by a person since deceased concerning the existence of a public right of way or a general right

available to a section of the public is admissible as evidence of the existence of such a right.

2. There are two conditions for admissibility:
   (a) the declarant must have had sufficient knowledge of the right; and
   (b) the declaration must have been made before any dispute concerning the right arose.

9.2.5 Declarations as to pedigree

Declarations as to date of birth, legitimacy, next of kin and the existence of a valid marriage are admissible providing:

1. the declaration must have been made by a deceased blood relative or spouse of a blood relative of the person in respect of whom the dispute had arisen; and
2. the declaration must have been made before the dispute arose.

The justification for this exception is that such a declaration may be the only evidence available.

9.3 STATEMENTS FORMING PART OF THE *RES GESTAE*

1. The doctrine of *res gestae* applies only in criminal cases.
2. A statement which forms part of the *res gestae* is one which is so closely connected with an incident in time, place and circumstance, as to form part of the same transaction.
3. *Res gestae* may be relevant in a number of circumstances, although the most popular use of the exception is where statements are made so close to the events leading to the charge that they cannot be separated from those events.
4. *Res gestae* can be a useful tool for admitting otherwise inadmissible hearsay statements.

9.3.1 Statements made in close association with unusual, startling or dramatic events

1. The *res gestae* doctrine allows for the admission of hearsay statements, whether or not the maker of the statement has since died.

2. The leading case is *R v Andrews* (1987), a House of Lords decision. The facts involved a victim who was stabbed by robbers in his flat. He was found by neighbours, badly injured, on the landing below. The police were summoned and the victim named his attackers. His statement was inadmissible as a dying declaration because there was no evidence that the victim was under a 'settled, hopeless expectation of death'. The House of Lords decided it was admissible as part of the *res gestae*.

3. Lord Ackner, in the course of his opinion, provides useful guidelines as to the circumstances in which *res gestae* statements will be admissible.

   (a) Spontaneity is an important factor: the statement must be so close to the events which led to the statement that the mind of the maker was still dominated by the event.

   (b) The event itself must provide the trigger for the statement. Lord Ackner makes clear that a statement will not necessarily be inadmissible where it is made in response to a question.

   (c) In considering whether to admit a statement under the *res gestae* doctrine, judges must consider any evidence advanced which suggests the deceased might have been motivated by malice against the defendant or might have been mistaken.

   (d) Excess alcohol, defective eyesight etc. will be relevant factors for consideration in deciding whether the evidence is likely to be free from error.

(e) Once the trial judge has ruled the evidence admissible, he must:

'make it clear to the jury that it is for them to decide what was said and to be sure that the witnesses were not mistaken in what they believed had been said to them.'

(f) Finally, Lord Ackner stressed that whilst the doctrine clearly admits statements where the maker remains alive (see *R v Glover* (1991)), prosecutors must not attempt to use *res gestae* as a device to avoid calling an available witness, since such a course would deprive the defence of the opportunity to cross-examine.

4. A useful comparison illustrating the application of the *res gestae* doctrine can be drawn between *R v Ney and Loan* (1977) and *Tobi v Nicholas* (1987).

(a) In *Ney and Loan*, a man named Lucas claimed he had been punched by the passenger of another vehicle following a collision. After the incident he had remained in his vehicle, shaken, until the police arrived within a short time and reported to the police what had happened. His statement was admitted as part of the *res gestae* because there had been no opportunity for concoction and no chance of error.

(b) In *Tobi v Nicholas* a collision occurred between a coach and a car. A police officer testified at the trial of the car driver that 20 minutes after the incident he went with the coach driver to a nearby house and saw a damaged car. He heard the coach driver identify the accused as the other driver. The conviction was quashed on appeal because the coach driver was not called to give evidence, and the accident was not so dramatic as to exclude the possibility of concoction.

9.3.2 Statements as to physical or mental state

1. Statements demonstrating the maker's physical state or state of mind at the time the statement was made may be

admitted as part of the *res gestae* provided the statement is:

(a) relevant; and

(b) contemporaneous.

2. This was explained in *Gilbey v Great Western Railway* (1910). Statements as to physical state are admissible as proof of a person's 'sensations at the time, about the pain in the side or head, or what not – whether those statements were made by groans or by actions or were verbal statements'.

3. A neighbour could testify, in a case alleging neglect of a child, that the child had complained of hunger on a recent occasion. Similarly, witnesses could testify as to fear, affection, dislike or pain where such physical states were relevant to the facts in issue.

4. A fairly recent illustration is *R v Gilfoyle* (1996). The defendant was convicted of murder. At trial, he claimed his wife had committed suicide, and indeed a suicide note, in his wife's hand, was found. The trial judge excluded the evidence of three witnesses who could have testified that shortly before her death, the wife had told them her husband was conducting a project on suicide and had persuaded her to write a suicide note. The Court of Appeal held that this evidence should have been admitted at trial. It was relevant to show her state of mind at the time the 'suicide note' was written, i.e. she was not suicidal, but believed she was helping her husband in his work.

9.3.3 Statements of intention

1. A statement of intention may be admissible to prove a person's intention at the time the statement was made.

2. It is much less certain whether such evidence will be admissible to prove that the maker of the statement went on to act in accordance with his expressed intentions.

3. Two cases illustrate the problem, and at first sight appear irreconcilable.

(a) In *R v Wainwright* (1875) evidence of a statement by the victim of murder that on leaving her lodgings, she intended to go to the premises of the accused, was held to be inadmissible. The evidence merely indicated her intention, which might not have been carried out.

(b) Conversely, in *R v Buckley* (1873) where the defendant was charged with murdering a policeman, the crucial issue was identity. A statement by the victim to a senior officer on the morning of the murder to the effect that he intended to watch the movements of the accused that night was held to be admissible.

4. A possible justification for the different results in these cases is that in *Buckley* the victim had explained to his superior officer how he proposed to utilise his working time. In those circumstances, he was professionally obliged to carry out his expressed intentions. In *Wainwright* there was no such obligation on the victim.

9.4 STATEMENTS IN PUBLIC DOCUMENTS

1. This common law exception is less important today than previously because of relatively recent enactments.

2. Statements in public documents will normally be admissible in criminal proceedings under s24 Criminal Justice Act 1988 (see Chapter 10).

3. In civil proceedings the common law exception is retained by s7(2) Civil Evidence Act 1995.

4. Statements in public documents are admissible as evidence of the truth of their contents (s7(2)(b)).

5. Conditions for admissibility are that:

(a) the document was compiled for public use and the public has access to it;

(b) the person making the record was acting under a public duty and compiled the document from personal knowledge;

(c) the record was compiled at a time when the maker might reasonably be expected to have a recollection of the events recorded; and

(d) the document was intended to form a permanent record.

CHAPTER 10

EXCEPTIONS TO THE HEARSAY RULE IN CRIMINAL CASES: STATUTORY EXCEPTIONS

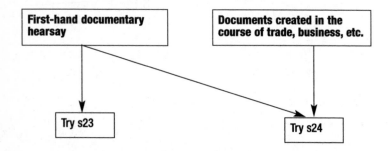

Statements contained in documents may be admissible as an exception to the hearsay rule under ss23 and 24 Criminal Justice Act 1988

First-hand documentary hearsay

Documents created in the course of trade, business, etc.

Try s23

Try s24

10.1 INTRODUCTION

Hearsay is admissible in criminal proceedings by virtue of the Criminal Justice Act 1988 (CJA 1988) and the Police and Criminal Evidence Act 1984 (PACE 1984):

- PACE 1984 governs the admission of confessions;
- ss23 and 24 CJA 1988 govern the admissibility of documentary hearsay in criminal cases other than confessions.

10.2 SECTION 23 CRIMINAL JUSTICE ACT 1988

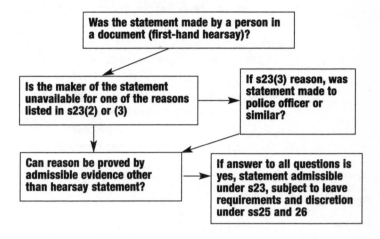

1. Section 23 CJA 1988 admits first-hand documentary hearsay in criminal trials.
   (a) Only statements 'made by a person in a document' are admissible, which means statements physically written down by the maker or dictated and checked by him. A person can also make a statement in a document by recording it onto a tape recorder, providing he knows the statement is being recorded.
   (b) *R v McGillivray* (1993) illustrates that a common-sense interpretation will be adopted. In that case a murder victim had dictated from his hospital bed a statement that was written down by a police officer in the presence of a nurse. Although the victim was unable to sign the statement because of his injuries, the court regarded it as a statement made by the victim.
2. A statement is only admissible under s23 where one of the statutory reasons for non-attendance listed in s23(2) or (3) applies. The first three reasons are listed in s23(2); the

fourth, at part (d), is contained in s23(3). Where the reason for non-attendance is fear, subsection (3) imposes an additional condition for admissibility.

(a) 'the person who made the statement is dead or by reason of his bodily or mental condition unable to attend as a witness'.

- 'Unable to attend' covers mental incapacity at the time of trial, so where a witness attends court but proves wholly unable to remember coherently, it may be possible to admit his statement (*R v Setz-Dempsey* (1994); *R v Ashford Justices ex parte Hilden* (1993)).

(b) '(i) the person who made the statement is outside the United Kingdom; and
(ii) it is not reasonably practicable to secure his attendance'.

- Before a statement can be admitted under s23(2)(b) the party wishing to rely on that statement must be able to prove not only that the witness normally resides abroad, but that the witness is physically outside the country at the time of trial and it is not reasonably practicable to secure his attendance (*R v Case* (1991); *R v Bray* (1988)).

(c) 'all reasonable steps have been taken to find the person who made the statement, but that he cannot be found.'

- Where the prosecution wishes to rely on the written statement of a witness who cannot now be found, they must first demonstrate the steps that have been taken to trace him.

(d) '(i) the statement was made to a police officer or some other person charged with the duty of investigating offences or charging offenders; and
(ii) the person who made it does not give oral evidence through fear or because he is kept out of the way.'

- It is not clear whether 'fear', under s23(3), is restricted to personal fear or extends to fear for others; whether it is restricted to fear of physical harm or fear of media attention, prosecution, or some other matter.

- The fear need not be based on reasonable grounds as long as it stems either from the commission of the offence or something said or done subsequently in relation to the offence, and relates to the possibility of the witness testifying as to the offence (*R v Martin* (1996)).

- Where the prosecutor wishes to admit evidence under this section, he must prove the existence of fear or that the witness has been kept out of the way to the criminal standard of proof. Where the defence makes such an assertion, the civil standard of proof is applicable.

3. If the prosecution wishes to rely on documentary hearsay under s23, they must have taken all reasonable steps to secure the attendance of the witness. Mere acceptance of a witness's professed refusal to attend may result in the statement's inadmissibility (*R v Gonzales de Orange* (1992)).

4. The admission of documentary hearsay under s23 is subject to the leave requirement under s26 and the general discretion to exclude under s25 (see section 10.4 below).

10.3 SECTION 24 CRIMINAL JUSTICE ACT 1988

Was the document created or received by a person acting in the course of trade, business, etc.?

↓

If information was passed through more than one person before being recorded: (i) did the supplier of information have personal knowledge of matters dealt with? (ii) did each person through whom information passed receive/record it in the course of trade businesses, etc.?

↓

If document was prepared for the purposes of criminal proceedings or investigation: Is the maker unavailable for reason listed in s23(2) or (3) OR Can maker of statement not reasonably be expected to have any recollection of matters dealt with?

↓

If answer to all questions is yes, statement admissible under s24, subject to leave requirement and discretion under ss25 and 26

1. Section 24(1) allows for the admission of documentary hearsay providing:
   (a) the person supplying the information had personal knowledge of the matters contained in the statement (s24(1)(ii)); and
   (b) the person compiling the document did so under a work-related duty (s24(1)(i)); and
   (c) any person through whom the information passed before reaching the compiler of the document was acting under a work-related duty in passing it on (s24(2)).

2. In *R v Rock* (1994) it was held that where messages for a customer were received by a paging company on to a hard copy and then copied out by an operator, the operator's copy was admissible under s24 as the operator had personal knowledge that someone was sending the message and was acting under a work-related duty in entering the message on the computer.

3. Section 24 does not make clear whether the *maker* of the statement is the person who supplies the information or the person who compiles the document. Case law suggests that either can be regarded as the maker (*R v Derodra* (2001)).

4. Subsection 3 specifically excludes confessions that would be inadmissible under s76 Police and Criminal Evidence Act 1984.

5. Subsection 4 imposes an additional condition where statements are prepared for the purposes of 'pending or contemplated criminal proceedings' or 'a criminal investigation': either one of the reasons for non-attendance listed in s23(2) or (3) applies or the additional reason included under s24(4)(iii):

    '(iii) the person who made the statement cannot reasonably be expected (having regard to the time which has elapsed since he made the statement and to all the circumstances) to have any recollection of the matters dealt with in the statement.'

6. In *R v Carrington* (1993) a party was allowed to select parts of a document and treat these as independent statements; thus where a statement contained a registration number, which the witness could not recollect, the part of the statement which contained that number could be treated as an independent statement for the purposes of s24(4)(iii), even though the witness could recollect other parts of the statement.

10.4 EXCLUSIONARY DISCRETION UNDER THE CRIMINAL JUSTICE ACT 1988

1. Section 25(1) CJA 1988 gives the judge a general discretion to exclude a statement admissible under s23 and s24 if, having regard to all the circumstances, he is of the opinion that the statement ought not to be admitted in the 'interests of justice'.

2. Subsection (2) explains the matters that judges must consider in exercising this discretion:

    '(a) ... the nature and source of the document containing the statement and to whether or not, having regard to its nature and source and to any other circumstances that appear to the court to be relevant, it is likely that the document is authentic;

    (b) ... the extent to which the statement appears to supply evidence which would otherwise not be readily available;

    (c) ... the relevance of the evidence that it appears to supply to any issue which is likely to have to be determined in the proceedings; and

    (d) ... any risk, having regard in particular to whether it is likely to be possible to controvert the statement if the person making it does not attend to give oral evidence in the proceedings, that its admission or exclusion will result in unfairness to the accused, or, if there is more than one, to any of them.'

10.5 LEAVE UNDER S26

1. Section 26 requires that a statement admissible under s23 or s24 for the purposes of pending or contemplated criminal proceedings or of a criminal investigation shall not be given in evidence without leave of the court.

2. Leave should not be given unless the court believes the statement 'ought to be admitted in the interests of justice'. In deciding whether to give leave, the court is required to have regard:

'(i) to the contents of the statement;

(ii) to any risk, having regard in particular to whether it is likely to be possible to controvert the statement if the person making it does not attend to give oral evidence in the proceedings, that its admission or exclusion will result in unfairness to the accused or, if there is more than one, to any of them; and

(iii) to any other circumstances that appear to the court to be relevant.'

3. The burden of proof differs under ss25 and 26:

(a) under s25 it is for the party opposing the admission of the evidence to establish that the interests of justice will be best served by exclusion of the statement;

(b) under s26 it is for the party wishing to tender evidence under ss23 or 24 to persuade the court that the statement should be admitted.

10.6 OTHER STATUTORY PROVISIONS IN CRIMINAL PROCEEDINGS

1. Section 60 Youth Justice and Criminal Evidence Act 1999 repeals s69 of PACE 1984 which 'ceases to have effect'. As a result, computerised documentary evidence is now governed by precisely the same rules as any other form of document, namely the person seeking to adduce it must prove to the requisite standard that:

(a) the document is authentic; and

(b) its contents are admissible.

2. So, if the document contains hearsay, its admission must be secured by bringing it within one of the exceptions to the

hearsay rule, for example s24 Criminal Justice Act 1988 (see *R v Derodra* (2001), in which a computerised crime report created by a police officer was admissible).

3. Note that with certain types of computer evidence, for example digital cameras, and computerised dialling systems, the computer is regarded as the 'perceiver' and hearsay problems do not arise.

4. Section 30 CJA 1988 admits written reports of expert witnesses, although the leave of the court is required if the expert does not attend.

5. Section 9 Criminal Justice Act 1967 applies to criminal proceedings in magistrates' and crown courts. It permits the admission of a witness statement provided:

   (a) it is properly signed;
   (b) it contains a declaration as to truth;
   (c) a copy is served on other parties;
   (d) none of the other parties serve notice objecting to the statement being tendered under s9.

10.7 HUMAN RIGHTS IMPLICATIONS

1. Whether or not the admission of hearsay evidence breaches the right to a fair trial under Article 6 European Convention on Human Rights, and in particular, the right under Article 6(3)(d) to 'examine or have examined' witnesses who provide evidence as part of the prosecution case at a criminal trial, is not entirely clear.

2. Decisions of the European Court of Human Rights have proved inconsistent on this issue:

   (a) in *Kostovski v The Netherlands* (1990) the ECtHR held that an accused must always be given 'adequate and proper opportunity to challenge and question a witness against him';

(b) in *Asch v Austria* (1993) the same court decided that there was no violation of convention rights unless the evidence of the absent witness constitutes the main part of the prosecution case.

3. It would seem that providing judges carefully apply the balancing exercise necessary under ss25 and 26 CJA 1988, excluding evidence from absent witnesses which forms the main plank of the prosecution case, courts are unlikely to conclude that s23 or s24 violates the terms of the HRA 1998.

4. This view finds support in the Court of Appeal decision, *R v Thomas and Flannagan* (1998). The trial judge had weighed very carefully the arguments on admissibility under s26 and gave a clear warning to the jury about the dangers of relying too heavily on the statement of a witness whose testimony had not been subjected to cross-examination. The court found no breach of Article 6(3).

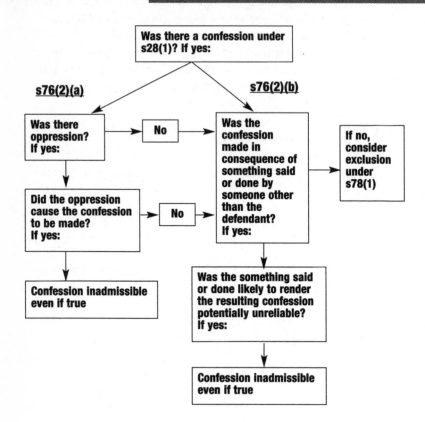

11.1 INTRODUCTION

1. An out-of-court confession will always be hearsay where the purpose of admitting it in evidence is to prove the truth of its contents.

2. Admissibility of confessions is governed by s76 PACE 1984, under which the prosecution has the legal burden of proving that the confession was not obtained by oppression

or by anything said or done which might render the confession unreliable.

3. Codes of Practice, created under the authority of PACE, but not part of the Act itself, provide guidance to police officers involved in the detention and interrogation of suspects.

4. Breaches of codes of practice do not render confessions automatically inadmissible, but may make it more difficult for the prosecution to prove admissibility under s76(2). Serious breaches may lead to exclusion of an otherwise admissible confession under s78(1).

11.2 SUMMARY OF CODE C OF CODES OF PRACTICE ISSUED UNDER PACE 1984

1. All persons in custody must be dealt with expeditiously, and released as soon as the need for detention has ceased to apply.

2. If an officer has any suspicion that a detained person of any age may be mentally disordered, or is under the age of 17, then he should not be interviewed without the presence of an 'appropriate adult'.

   (a) In the case of juveniles this will normally be a parent or guardian, but may be a social worker or other responsible person over the age of 18.

   (b) In the case of a mentally disordered suspect, a relative, social worker experienced in dealing with mental disorders, or some other responsible adult must be present.

3. All persons detained must be informed of their right to receive free legal advice and must not normally (subject to exceptions) be interviewed until legal advice has been received.

4. No police officer should at any time do or say anything with the intention of dissuading a person in detention from obtaining legal advice.

5. Any person detained at a police station who is not under arrest must be informed of his right to leave the police station at any time.

6. Any person arrested and held in custody at a police station is entitled to have one person informed of his whereabouts at public expense.

7. Cells must be adequately heated, cleaned, ventilated and lit, and no additional restraints can normally be used within a locked cell, other than handcuffs where absolutely necessary.

8. Regular meals and drinks must be provided and, where necessary, advice on diet must be sought from a police doctor.

9. Juveniles must not normally be detained in a cell unless no other secure accommodation is available, and in any event, must not be placed in a cell with a detained adult.

10. A person suspected of having committed an offence must be cautioned before any questions are asked.

11. Where an appropriate adult is present at an interview, he should be informed as to the nature of his role: to advise the person being questioned; to observe whether the interview is being conducted properly and fairly; to facilitate communication.

12. Breaks from interviewing must take place at recognised meal times and short refreshment breaks must normally be provided at approximately two-hourly intervals.

11.3 DEFINITION OF 'CONFESSION'

1. The partial definition of 'confession' in PACE is that '"confession" includes any statement wholly or partly adverse to the person who made it, whether made to a person in authority or not and whether made in words or otherwise' (s82(1)).

2. A recent case illustrates that even a relatively simple definition can give rise to problems of interpretation. **Example**: In *R v Ward, Andrews and Broadley* (2001) the three appellants were convicted of a conspiracy to steal from motor vehicles. Part of the prosecution case consisted of evidence that on three occasions a car had been stopped, and one of the passengers identified himself as Ward and gave Ward's correct date of birth and address. The attendant police officer was later unable to identify Ward as the passenger. Ward's appeal was based on the fact that this evidence was hearsay and should not have been admitted. It was held that the evidence was admissible under s76 as a confession, because the statement was adverse to the defendant's interest. This is not a decision that will attract universal approval. If the statement was indeed hearsay (and that is debateable), it could surely only be adverse to the maker if proved to have been made by Ward?

11.4 ADMISSIBILITY UNDER s76

1. A confession is admissible against its maker (and not others) as evidence of the truth of its contents (s76(1)).
2. Admissibility may be raised by the defence, or the court itself may, under s76(3), require the prosecution to prove that the confession was not obtained by the methods described in subsection (2).
3. Admissibility will be decided following a *voir dire* and the burden of proof is on the prosecution to prove that the confession is admissible.
4. PACE and the Codes of Practice issued under PACE contain many provisions re arrest, detention, treatment and questioning of suspects. Breach of these rules does not necessarily mean that any resulting confession was obtained by the methods in subsection (2), but MAY do so either alone or with other evidence, or may result in the exclusion of the confession in the exercise of the court's discretion under s78(1).

11.4.1 Oppression under s76(2)(a)

1. Where the prosecution is unable to prove that a confession was not obtained 'by oppression' (s76(2)(a)), the confession will be inadmissible, whether or not it is also considered unreliable.

2. It is only inadmissible where it is made 'as a result' of oppression, so if the confession is made **before** any oppressive conduct, it will be admissible.

3. (a) s76(8) defines oppression as 'including torture, inhuman or degrading treatment, and the use or threat of violence (whether or not amounting to torture)'.

   (b) However, this statutory definition is not used in practice. Instead, the Court of Appeal preferred the ordinary dictionary definition of oppression in *R v Fulling* (1987): 'the exercise of authority or power in a burdensome, harsh or wrongful manner, unjust or cruel treatment of subjects, inferiors etc; the imposition of unreasonable or unjust burdens'.

4. *R v Beales* (1991) and *R v Glaves* (1993) provide examples of oppressive conduct leading to the exclusion of confessions. In *Beales* the court found that the defendant had been 'hectored and bullied from first to last'. In *Glaves* the defendant, aged 16, was subjected to an oppressive interview without an appropriate adult being present.

5. Perhaps the most worrying example of oppressive interrogation techniques is provided by *R v Paris, Abdullahi and Miller* (1993): interviews were held over five days and lasted some 13 hours. The suspect in question had an IQ of 75, just on the borderline of mental handicap. Lord Taylor CJ said:

   'Having denied involvement well over 300 times, he was finally persuaded to make admissions... [He] was bullied and hectored. The officers... were not questioning him so much as shouting at him what they wanted him to say.

Short of physical violence, it is hard to conceive of a more hostile and intimidating approach by officers to a suspect.'

6. Few confessions will be declared inadmissible under s76(2)(a), and as the cases above illustrate, only where interrogation techniques cross the boundaries of police propriety.

7. *R v Miller* (1986) quite clearly demonstrates that s76(2) is concerned with technical admissibility, not weight or credibility of confessions: the appellant was a paranoid schizophrenic who had confessed to murder. Parts of the confession were consistent with known facts whilst other parts were pure fantasy. It was held that the fact the police interviews might unintentionally have caused hallucinations was not oppression. The confession was admissible.

8. Conduct which has been held to fall short of oppression includes loss of patience and bad language on the part of a police officer (*R v Emmerson* (1990)) and uncomfortable, cold conditions accompanied by a minor breach of the Code of Practice (*R v Hughes* (1988)).

11.4.2 Unreliability under s76(2)(b)

1. 'Unreliability' must also be given its ordinary dictionary definition: 'cannot be relied upon, untrustworthy or unsafe'.

2. Judges must adopt a subjective approach, taking on board the characteristics of the accused in deciding whether a confession is unreliable.

3. Judges must assess the **potential** unreliability of the confession, not its **actual** unreliability. It would not therefore be appropriate for a judge to consider the truth of a confession in deciding admissibility under s76(2)(b).

4. Unreliability does not require police impropriety (see *R v Sat-Bhambra* (1988)). At the same time, 'things said or done' may be illegal, or in breach of the Act yet not render

the confession unreliable where, for example, the accused is an experienced professional criminal (*R v Alladice* (1998)).

5. An example of a confession being excluded under s76(2)(b) is *R v Harvey* (1988). A woman with low intelligence, and who was suffering from a psychopathic disorder, confessed when told by police officers that her lover had confessed. Although there was nothing improper in the conduct of the interview, the Court of Appeal held that the confession might have been a child-like attempt to protect her lover, and was therefore potentially unreliable.

6. Interviewing a juvenile or a person suffering from a mental disorder in the absence of an appropriate adult, or refusing access to legal advice, may be construed as the 'something said or done' which renders a confession unreliable (see *R v Morse and Others* (1991); *R v Blake* (1989); *R v McGovern* (1991)).

7. More confessions are declared inadmissible for unreliability under s76(2)(b) than for oppression under s76(2)(a), nevertheless, it should be noted that the statutory test is strictly applied.

8. The cases of *R v Goldenburg* (1988) and *R v Crampton* (1991), where each of the two defendants was a heroin addict, suffering withdrawal at the time of making his confession, illustrate that courts will not declare confessions inadmissible under s76(2)(b) purely because they are potentially unreliable: such confessions must be unreliable 'in consequence of anything said or done' by a third party.

11.5 DISCRETION TO EXCLUDE AN OTHERWISE ADMISSIBLE CONFESSION AT COMMON LAW AND UNDER S78(1)

Confession evidence can be excluded either at common law or under s78(1) Police and Criminal Evidence Act 1984.

11.5.1 Discretion at common law

1. Section 82(3) states: 'Nothing in this part of this Act shall prejudice any power of a court to exclude evidence (whether by preventing questions from being put or otherwise) at its discretion.'

2. This section preserves the common law power of a judge to exclude confession evidence, although the more recent statutory power under s78 is preferred today.

3. Common law powers to exclude confessions were used prior to PACE in three situations:
   (a) where the probative value of the confession was outweighed by its prejudicial effect (*R v Stewart* (1972));
   (b) where it was obtained by improper or unfair means;
   (c) where it was obtained in breach of Codes of Practice or the statutory provisions governing the detention and treatment of suspects.

4. The common-law discretion remains useful in just one situation: where a judge admits a confession following a *voir dire*, but later changes his view having heard the whole of the evidence, the common law power allows him to direct the jury to disregard the confession. Section 78(1) entitles a judge to exclude evidence 'on which the prosecution **proposes** to rely', and evidence cannot be retrospectively excluded once it has been adduced in open court.

11.5.2 Discretion under s78(1)

1. Section 78(1) states that 'In any proceedings the court may refuse to allow evidence on which the prosecution proposes to rely to be given if it appears to the court that, having regard to all the circumstances, including the circumstances in which the evidence was obtained, the admission of the evidence would have such an adverse effect on the fairness of the proceedings that the court ought not to admit it'.

2. This section extends to all prosecution evidence, not just confessions. It tends to be used quite commonly as a sanction against the police, although potentially it has a much wider use.

3. *R v Mason* (1987) remains the leading case on exclusion of confession evidence. The accused confessed to arson having been told by police officers that his fingerprints had been found at the scene. This was a lie designed to elicit a confession. The Court of Appeal held that the confession should have been excluded under s78(1).

4. Confession evidence may be excluded where a suspect detained for questioning at a police station is improperly denied access to legal advice.

5. The courts often look at the motives of the police officers in deciding whether or not to exercise discretion:

   (a) where they have acted in 'bad faith', a confession will be excluded; where they have acted in 'good faith' it will not;

   (b) in *R v Alladice* (1988) the Lord Chief Justice stated: 'If the police have acted in bad faith the court will have little difficulty in ruling any confession inadmissible under s78, if not under s76 ... If the police, albeit in good faith, have nevertheless fallen foul of s58, it is still necessary for the court to decide whether to admit the evidence would adversely affect the fairness of the proceedings, and would do so to such an extent that the confession ought to be excluded.';

   (c) but in *R v Samuel* (1988) it was made plain that this test will not be appropriate in all circumstances.

6. *R v Brine* (1992) illustrates that s78 is not concerned exclusively with misconduct by the police. The accused was suffering from a mild paranoid psychosis which would have made him feel threatened by questioning and prone to lie and falsely confess. There had been nothing said or done by the police which would render the confession unreliable

under s76(2)(b), but the Court of Appeal held that s78 should have been used to exclude the confession on the grounds of fairness.

7. In *R v Quinn* (1990), it was explained that the function of the judge is to protect the fairness of the proceedings, and normally proceedings will be fair if a jury hears all relevant evidence which either side wishes to place before it, but proceedings may become unfair if, for example:
   - one side is allowed to adduce relevant evidence which, for one reason or another, the other side cannot properly challenge or meet; or
   - where there has been an abuse of process, e.g. because evidence has been obtained in deliberate breach of procedures laid down in an official code of practice.

8. In the absence of any misdirection by the trial judge, the Court of Appeal will be reluctant to interfere with the exercise of discretion.

11.6 CONFESSIONS BY THE MENTALLY HANDICAPPED

1. Mental handicap is relevant both to admissibility under s76(2) and to discretion to exclude a confession either at common law or under s78(1).

2. Whilst Code C provides pre-trial protection by requiring the presence of an 'appropriate adult' at any interview with a mentally disordered person, s77(1) provides additional protection at trial.

3. Section 77(1) imposes a statutory responsibility on judges to warn a jury of the need for caution before relying upon a confession by a mentally handicapped person where the court is satisfied that:
   - he is mentally handicapped; and
   - the confession was not made in the presence of an independent person.

4. It is for the defence to establish on a balance of probabilities that the circumstances set out in s77(1) apply.

5. Section 77(3) defines mental handicap as 'a state of arrested or incomplete development of mind which includes significant impairment of intelligence and social functioning'.

6. Lord Taylor CJ provided further guidance to judges dealing with confessions by the mentally handicapped in the case of *R v McKenzie* (1993), saying: 'Where
   (i) the prosecution case depends wholly upon confessions, and
   (ii) the accused suffers from a significant degree of mental handicap; and
   (iii) the confessions are unconvincing to a point where a jury properly directed could not properly convict upon them,

   then the judge, assuming he has not excluded the confessions earlier, should withdraw the case from the jury.'

11.7 FACTS DISCOVERED AS A RESULT OF AN INADMISSIBLE CONFESSION

1. At common law, incriminating facts discovered as a result of an inadmissible confession were admissible (*R v Warwickshall* (1783)).

2. The common rule was given statutory force and clarification under s76(4) and (5) of PACE:

3. Evidence that a fact was discovered as a result of an inadmissible confession made by the accused cannot be led by the prosecution, but remains admissible if led by the accused or his counsel (s76(4)(a) and (5)).

4. Under s76(4)(b), where something in an inadmissible confession shows that the accused speaks, writes or expresses himself in a particular manner, and this serves to

identify him as the offender, that part of the confession is admissible as non-hearsay evidence: the purpose of admitting it is not to prove the truth of the words, simply to show the manner of writing or speaking.

5. Section 76(4) and (5) apply to confessions which are inadmissible under s76.

6. If a confession is excluded under s78, then the common law rules apply (point 1 above).

11.8 PROPOSALS FOR REFORM OF THE HEARSAY RULE

1. Clause 98 of the Criminal Justice Bill 2002 proposes radical reform of the present hearsay rules. Under the draft legislation, hearsay will be admissible in four circumstances:
   (a) where it is admissible under a statutory provision;
   (b) where it is admissible under a common law rule preserved by the Bill (it would appear that all those common law exceptions dealt with in Chapter 9 are retained, with the exception of dying declarations);
   (c) where the parties agree to its admission;
   (d) where the court gives leave to admit the statement.

2. Before deciding to give leave to admit a statement under (d) above, the court must first be satisfied that the admission of the hearsay evidence would not be contrary to the interests of justice. Factors which must be considered include:
   (a) the degree of relevance of the statement in proving a matter in issue;
   (b) the circumstances in which it was made;
   (c) the extent to which it supplies evidence not otherwise available;
   (d) the creditworthiness of the maker;
   (e) the reason why oral evidence cannot be given;
   (f) the extent to which the other party can challenge the statement and the risk of unfairness.

3. Potentially, the new proposed exception to the hearsay rule extends to multiple hearsay as well as first-hand hearsay.

4. Confessions will only be admissible if they meet the additional requirements of s76 PACE 1984.

5. Where a witness is unavailable to give evidence, both oral and documentary first-hand hearsay will be admissible if one of the reasons listed in clause 100 exists, i.e. the witness is:
   (a) dead;
   (b) ill;
   (c) absent abroad;
   (d) disappeared; or
   (e) in fear.

6. Before evidence can be admitted under clause 100, the witness must be identified to the court's satisfaction, and the opposing party will have the opportunity to challenge the absent witness's credibility.

7. Clause 101 deals with business related documents and broadly adopts the rules currently contained with s24 Criminal Justice Act 1988 (Chapter 10). The only proposed change is:
   - the hearsay statement will be admissible only if the supplier of the information is unavailable or cannot reasonably be expected to recall the matters dealt with in the statement.

CHAPTER 12

EVIDENCE OBTAINED BY ILLEGAL OR UNFAIR MEANS

<u>General rule</u>: evidence is admissible even where it is obtained illegally or unfairly, but may be excluded under the exercise of judicial discretion.

<u>Exclusion at common law</u>
- where probative value is outweighed by prejudicial effect
- confession evidence
- evidence obtained from accused after commision of offence

<u>Exclusion under s78 PACE</u>
Where the admission of evidence would have such an adverse effect on the fairness of the proceedings that it ought not to be admitted

12.1 THE GENERAL RULE

1. There is no general rule excluding relevant evidence on the grounds that it was obtained illegally or improperly (for example, by means of a crime, trickery, deception or as a result of inducements). The only two exceptions to that rule relate to:
   - privileged documents (see section 14.5); and
   - confessions (see section 11.4).

2. The clearest statement of the common law position was delivered by Crompton J in *R v Leatham* (1861):
   'It matters not how you get it; if you steal it even, it would be admissible in evidence.'

3. In *Kuruma v R* (1955), where evidence was discovered in the course of an illegal search, it remained admissible, despite the fact that the search produced evidence of a capital offence.

4. At the other end of the spectrum, in *Jeffrey v Black* (1978) the defendant was suspected of stealing a sandwich. An illegal search of his home revealed a quantity of cannabis and he was charged with possession. The Court of Appeal held that the Magistrates' Court had erroneously excluded that evidence.

12.2 DISCRETION TO EXCLUDE AT COMMON LAW

1. Section 82(3) PACE 1984 retains the common law discretion to exclude admissible evidence, although its scope remains unclear, despite a House of Lords ruling in *R v Sang* (1980), which attempted to lay down guidelines.

   (a) Lord Diplock explained the general rule and the role of the judge to ensure fairness, but that
   'What the judge at the trial is concerned with is not how the evidence sought to be adduced by the prosecution has been obtained, but with how it is used by the prosecution at trial'.

   (b) Viscount Dilhorne outlined the purpose of the common law discretion to exclude evidence by saying:
   'It is not the manner in which [the evidence] has been obtained but its use at the trial if accompanied by prejudicial effects outweighing its probative value and so rendering the trial unfair to the accused which will justify the exercise of judicial discretion to exclude it'.

   (c) More confusingly, Lord Diplock emphasised that although a trial judge has discretion to exclude evidence where its prejudicial effect outweighs its probative value, the only common law discretion to exclude evidence relates to confession evidence, 'and … evidence obtained from the accused after commission of the offence'.

2. Few people claim to fully understand the ambit of the discretion as explained by the House of Lords in *R v Sang,*

however, since the enactment of PACE, the common law discretion has become virtually redundant, with little, if any, distinction remaining between the two.

12.3 DISCRETION TO EXCLUDE UNDER s78(1) PACE 1984

1. Section 78(1) states that: 'In any proceedings the court may refuse to allow evidence on which the prosecution proposes to rely to be given if it appears to the court that, having regard to all the circumstances, including the circumstances in which the evidence was obtained, the admission of the evidence would have such an adverse effect on the fairness of the proceedings that the court ought not to admit it.'

2. To date the power has not been used rigorously as a judicial tool to strengthen individual rights or maintain standards of propriety.

3. It is possible that s78(1) will be used more widely in the future in light of the new responsibilities imposed upon judges under s6 Human Rights Act 1998, although the evidence to date is not suggestive of a more proactive use.

4. As was considered above at section 11.5.2, some judges appear to operate a good faith/bad faith test, using s78(1) to exclude evidence obtained illegally and in bad faith. This approach is illustrated by the cases of *Matto v Crown Court at Wolverhampton* (1987) and *Fox v Chief Constable of Gwent* (1986). Both cases involved the unlawful administration of a breath test to drivers suspected of driving with excess alcohol.

   (a) In *Matto*, the officers knew they were acting unlawfully, and the Court of Appeal held that the evidence relating to the test should have been excluded under s78(1).

   (b) Conversely, in *Fox*, officers believed, erroneously, that they were acting within the law. The Court of Appeal held that the evidence had been properly admitted.

5. The case of *R v Khan* (1997), which was considered by the Court of Appeal, the House of Lords and the European Court of Human Rights is regarded by many as disappointing in its failure to expand the use of s78(1) to strengthen human rights. Evidence was obtained by police officers using an unlawful surveillance technique, in contravention of Article 8 European Convention – the right to privacy. It was conceded by the prosecution that, in the absence of any lawful authorisation, this form of covert surveillance amounted to a civil trespass. Nevertheless, all three courts found that the evidence obtained as a result of this unlawful operation was properly admitted at Khan's trial.

12.4 ENTRAPMENT

1. 'Entrapment' means enticement to commit an offence that would not have been committed in the absence of enticement.
2. Undercover operations by police officers who have infiltrated criminal gangs in an attempt to gather information and evidence is not entrapment.
3. The courts will not generally be prepared to exercise discretion under s78(1) to exclude evidence obtained in the course of undercover operations but they may be prepared to do so where an offence is procured by means of entrapment.

Examples

(a) In *R v Christou* (1992), where police set up a jewellery shop visited by the Defendant in an attempt to sell stolen jewellery, tape recordings of incriminatory conversations were not excluded by the court, since the defendant had not been tricked into committing an offence.

(b) In *R v Smurthwaite* (1994) the defendant had sought to arrange the murder of his wife through an undercover police officer posing as a contract killer. Tape recordings of the conversations were properly admitted at trial since the operation involved no entrapment.

4. Guidance from the European Court of Human Rights was provided in the case of *Texeira de Castro v Portugal* (1999) where it was said:

   'The general requirements of fairness embodied in Art. 6 apply to proceedings concerning all types of criminal offence, from the most straightforward to the most complex. The public interest cannot justify the use of evidence obtained as a result of police incitement.'

5. Merely giving a defendant an opportunity to break the law is not entrapment (*Nottingham City Council v Amin* (2001)).

6. *R v Loosely* (2001) suggests that future cases will be decided on the basis of the abuse of process doctrine rather than s78(1). The effect of a successful abuse of process application would be the collapse of the prosecution case.

7. Applying the new 'abuse of process' approach to the cases discussed above, it is unlikely that a different decision would be reached. However in *R v Shannon* (2001) where there was clear evidence that the defendant was persuaded or pressurised into committing the offence, the Court of Appeal did consider applying the abuse of process doctrine.

8. As a result of *Loosely* it is likely that future courts, on similar facts, would exclude such evidence as an abuse of process without the need to consider its effect upon the fairness of the trial under s78(1).

CHAPTER 13

OPINION EVIDENCE

Admission of expert evidence

CRIMINAL CASES	**CIVIL CASES**
Documentary evidence admissible under s30(1) Criminal Justice Act 1988	Admissibility governed by Part 35 CPR and relevant Practice Direction
Must relate to issue beyond normal competence of court and necessary to aid understanding	Under s3(2) Civil Evidence Act 1972, expert may testify on any relevant matter within his expertise
Court must be satisfied as to witness's status as expert	Judges, as case managers, regulate extent and nature of expert evidence
Testimony must be based upon the admissible facts in the particular case	Judge must have regard to overriding objective, focusing on cost and proportionality

13.1 INTRODUCTION

1. The general rule is that opinion evidence is inadmissible in both criminal and civil cases: witnesses can testify only as to matters of fact within their own personal knowledge.

2. Exceptions to this rule are:
   (a) witnesses are allowed to give statements of opinion based on their own personal knowledge and not calling for special expertise;
   (b) witnesses who satisfy the court of their 'expert' status are allowed to give opinion evidence within their field of expertise;
   (c) in civil cases opinion evidence relating to matters of public concern and family history is admissible.

13.2 ADMISSION OF OPINION EVIDENCE NOT CALLING FOR SPECIAL EXPERTISE

1. Where a lay witness forms an opinion, based upon his personal knowledge, he will be allowed to testify as to that opinion.
2. In a criminal case, such a statement is admissible at common law; in a civil case it is admissible under s3(2) Civil Evidence Act 1972.
3. This sort of evidence is admitted routinely at trial: any witness who gives evidence relating to identity is, in effect, giving opinion evidence.

13.3 ADMISSION OF EVIDENCE CALLING FOR SPECIAL EXPERTISE

13.3.1 Criminal cases

1. There is no exhaustive list of issues upon which expert testimony will be allowed.
2. Forensic testimony is commonly admitted to prove a defendant's presence at a crime scene. This may take the form of fingerprint evidence, DNA, bloodstains, fibres, footprints, tyre prints, handwriting, etc.

3. Other issues on which expert testimony has been allowed include:
   - psychological evidence when considering a defence of diminished responsibility or insanity (*R v Ahluwalia* (1992));
   - psychological effects on children of 'battle cards', given away free with chewing gum (*DPP v ABC Chewing Gum* (1968));
   - changes to the stock market;
   - foreign law;
   - artistic merit ;
   - facial mapping;
   - voice identification; and virtually any other issue outside the ordinary competence of the court.

4. A written report from an expert witness is admissible under s30(1) Criminal Justice Act 1988, whether or not the expert is called to testify in person.

5. Leave would be required under s25 where the prosecution proposes to admit the report without calling the witness, and this is likely to be refused where the report is challenged by the defence.

6. Admissibility depends upon two factors:
   (a) it must relate to an issue that goes beyond the normal competence of the court and must be necessary to aid the court in understanding the issue or reaching a decision on the facts;
   (b) before expert evidence can be admitted at trial, the court must be satisfied as to the witness's status as an expert and this will involve a consideration of his qualifications and experience. The burden of proof in establishing expertise lies with the party seeking to call the witness. *R v Silverlock* (1894) illustrates that expertise need not be attained in the course of a profession and an 'expert' need not possess formal qualifications.

7. Expert testimony must be based upon the facts in a particular case, and those facts must themselves be admissible in evidence (*R v Turner* (1975)).

8. *Turner* establishes that expert evidence is inadmissible:
   (a) when it concerns an issue within the knowledge and experience of the jury;
   (b) when it concerns an issue of human nature and behaviour within the bounds of normality.

9. Where a defence of diminished responsibility under s2 Homicide Act 1957 is raised, expert evidence will invariably be admitted because the court or jury is unlikely to have sufficient knowledge of mental abnormality to reach a safe conclusion without help (*R v Dix* (1982)).

13.3.2 The admission of evidence calling for special expertise in civil cases

1. In civil cases, the nature of admissible expert evidence is just as varied as in criminal cases.

2. Admissibility is governed by Part 35 Civil Procedure Rules (CPR 35) and the relevant Practice Direction to Part 35.

3. In an attempt to eradicate the pre-Woolf 'battle of the experts' problems associated with expert testimony, judges have assumed responsibility for regulating the extent and nature of expert evidence under their new role as case managers.

4. Expert witnesses today owe an overriding duty to the court, not to the party who calls and pays them.

5. On the small-claims track, expert evidence will rarely be admissible; on the fast-track, such evidence may be restricted to the admission of written reports; on the multi-track, the judge may rule that one agreed expert be called instead of each party calling its own witness. Where the parties cannot agree upon a common expert, the court has power to appoint an expert of its choosing.

6. A judge must have regard to the overriding objective to deal with each case justly, and this requires him to focus on cost and proportionality, bearing in mind the value of the claim.

7. Section 3(2) Civil Evidence Act 1972 governs the nature of admissible expert evidence:
'where a person is called as a witness in civil proceedings, his opinion on any relevant matter on which he is qualified to give expert evidence, shall be admissible ...'

8. CPR 35 states:
'Expert evidence should be restricted to that which is reasonably required to resolve the proceedings.'

13.4 OPINION EVIDENCE ON MATTERS OF PUBLIC CONCERN AND FAMILY HISTORY

1. A third exception allowing for the admission of non-expert opinion evidence exists by virtue of a common law rule, which was preserved by s7(3) Civil Evidence Act 1995. This allows for evidence relating to such matters as family history, reputation, or the existence of a marriage.

2. The weight accorded to such evidence will be a matter for the court to decide.

13.5 TESTIFYING AS TO THE ULTIMATE ISSUE

1. At common law, experts were not entitled to give evidence as to the ultimate issue, i.e. the defendant's guilt or innocence. Witnesses were required to circumvent the rule by choosing their words carefully.

2. The case of *R v Stockwell* (1995) effectively witnessed the final demise of this rule, when an expert in facial mapping testified that, based on the measurements he had taken

from the security video and the defendant's face, there was strong evidence to suggest that the defendant was the person depicted on the videotape. It is generally recognised today that this rule has little relevance.

3. The modern position is that an expert can testify as to the ultimate issue providing the jury is directed that they are not required to accept the opinion of the expert on that matter.

4. In civil cases, the ultimate issue will involve the question of liability. Whereas, historically, experts were not permitted to testify as to the ultimate issue in civil cases, s3(1) Civil Evidence Act 1972 does provide for the admission of opinion evidence on 'any relevant matter'. The ultimate issue is arguably the most relevant issue before the court, hence it is generally accepted that s3(1) has supplanted the common law rule. The court today is free to accord whatever weight it feels appropriate to the evidence of an expert witness on the ultimate issue.

CHAPTER 14

DISCLOSURE AND THE EXCLUSION OF EVIDENCE ON THE GROUNDS OF PRIVILEGE AND PUBLIC POLICY

Disclosure of evidence

CRIMINAL CASES

Regulated by ss3–5 Criminal Procedure and Investigations Act 1996

↓

Primary disclosure: prosecutor must disclose material which might undermine prosecution case (s3(1))

↓

Defence disclosure: nature of defence, matters upon which issue is taken with prosecution case with reasons (s5(6))

↓

Secondary prosecution disclosure: all material which might reasonably be expected to assist the defence

CIVIL CASES

Multi-track and fast track proceedings regulated by Part 31 Civil Procedure Rules

Each party to disclose:
- documents relied on;
- documents adversely affecting own or other party's case;
- documents supporting opponent's case;
- all documents requiring disclosure under Practice Direction

14.1 INTRODUCTION

1. The general rule in both criminal and civil proceedings is that all relevant evidence is admissible.

(a) In criminal cases the rule is given statutory force under the Criminal Procedure and Investigations Act 1996 (outlined briefly at section 14.2 below).

(b) In civil proceedings on the fast track and multi-track, disclosure is governed by Part 31 Civil Procedure Rules and the substance of that rule will be considered below at section 14.3.

2. Despite the statutory duties to disclose relevant evidence, exceptions exist both in criminal and civil cases. In criminal cases, a number of exceptions have already been considered:

- confession evidence is admissible only if it accords with the conditions for admissibility laid down by s76(2) PACE 1984;
- all relevant evidence is subject to the common law and statutory discretions to exclude evidence in the interests of fairness;
- previous criminal convictions of defendants are normally excluded by virtue of s1(3) Criminal Evidence Act 1898;
- hearsay evidence is normally inadmissible unless it falls within one of the exceptions to the rule.

3. In addition, evidence may be excluded, despite its relevance, in both criminal and civil cases, where it is privileged, or on the grounds of public policy. These exceptions are considered below (sections 14.3–14.7).

14.2 DISCLOSURE

14.2.1 Criminal cases

1. The Criminal Procedure and Investigations Act 1996 imposed statutory requirements upon both prosecution and defence for the disclosure of evidence at a pre-trial stage.

2. In summary, the disclosure requirements under the Act consist of four elements:

(i) there is a **statutory duty upon the investigating officer to record and retain information** and material gathered in the course of an investigation;

(ii) **primary disclosure:** 'the prosecutor must ... disclose to the accused any prosecution material which... in the prosecutor's opinion might undermine the case for the prosecution against the accused' (s3(l)(a));

(iii) once the prosecution has complied with the duty of primary disclosure, this triggers **defence disclosure**: 'in general terms the nature of the accused's defence [must be disclosed] ... indicating the matters on which he takes issue with the prosecution and setting out in the case of each such matter the reason why he takes issue with the prosecution'. The defence statement must include details of any alibi, together with names and addresses of witnesses, where known. This statement must be issued within 14 days of primary disclosure being made;

(iv) **secondary disclosure** by the prosecution need be made only once the defence obligation has been complied with. At that point the prosecution must disclose 'material which might reasonably be expected to assist the defence'.

3. Failure by the defence to disclose in accordance with s5, any inconsistency between the statement and the defence presented at trial, late disclosure, or use of an alibi or alibi witnesses without providing details in the statement may lead to comment by the prosecution and/or a co-accused, and allow *proper* inferences to be drawn in determining the issue of guilt.

4. In November 2000 the Attorney-General, following wide consultation with all parties, issued guidelines on disclosure designed to minimise potential abuse and prevent miscarriages of justice. The guidelines introduced the following safeguards:

   ● that investigations should always err on the side of recording and retaining material when there is any doubt as to its relevance;

   ● where large quantities of evidence are seized by investigators as a precautionary measure, without any intention to examine such evidence in detail, the existence of such evidence should be made known to the accused in general terms at the primary stage and permission granted for its inspection by him or his legal advisors.

5. In *R v Vasilou* (2000), the prosecution's failure to disclose to the defence that its three main witnesses had previous criminal convictions, led to the quashing of the appellant's conviction and the ordering of a retrial.

14.2.2 Reform to disclosure rules in criminal cases

1. Part 5 Criminal Justice Bill 2002 proposes reform to disclosure rules in criminal cases.

2. Clause 27 amends s3 CPIA 1996, introducing a new objective single test for the disclosure of unused prosecution material. It replaces both primary and secondary disclosure requirements.

3. The new test will require the prosecution to disclose: 'any prosecution material which has not previously been disclosed to the accused and which might reasonably be considered capable of undermining the case for the prosecution against the accused, or of assisting the case for the accused.'

4. Clause 28 repeals the current requirement for defence disclosure contained within ss6–9 CPIA 1996. Under the Criminal Justice Bill the defendant will be required to provide a more detailed defence statement and to notify the prosecution of any points of law he wishes to rely on at trial.

5. Clause 29 will require the defendant to notify the prosecution of his intention to call defence witnesses and furnish the names, addresses and dates of birth for such witnesses.

6. The prosecution's duty to disclose unused material to the defendant will continue from the time of initial disclosure until the end of the trial.

14.2.3 Disclosure in civil cases

1. In civil proceedings, on the multi-track and fast track, Part 31 Civil Procedure Rules lays down standard disclosure requirements.
2. On the small claims track, disclosure is required only in respect of evidence relied on at trial.
3. Rule 31.6 requires each party to disclose:
   - documents upon which he relies;
   - documents which adversely affect his case;
   - documents which adversely affect another party's case;
   - documents which support another party's case; and
   - all documents required to be disclosed under a Practice Direction.

14.3 INTRODUCTION TO PRIVILEGE

There are three types of privilege that may give rise to the exclusion of relevant evidence:
- the privilege against self-incrimination;
- legal professional privilege; and
- 'without prejudice' negotiations.

14.4 THE PRIVILEGE AGAINST SELF-INCRIMINATION

1. The privilege against self-incrimination applies in both criminal and civil proceedings and entitles witnesses to refuse to answer questions or to produce relevant documents in circumstances where such evidence might give rise to a criminal charge or criminal sanction.
2. The privilege belongs to the witness and must be claimed by that witness during the course of testimony.
3. Where the privilege is not claimed, incriminatory answers remain admissible and may be used in criminal proceedings against the witness.

4. The ambit of the rule was explained in *Blunt v Park Lane Hotel* (1942):

   'The rule is that no-one is bound to answer any question if the answer thereto would, in the opinion of the judge, have a tendency to expose [him] to any criminal charge or penalty which the judge regards as reasonably likely to be preferred or sued for.'

5. A witness may refuse to answer questions that might incriminate his/her spouse. This privilege is recognised in criminal proceedings and has statutory force in civil proceedings under s14(1)(b) Civil Evidence Act 1968. It should be noted that the privilege is that of the witness, not the spouse, and if the witness chooses to answer questions of an incriminatory nature, s/he is entitled to do so.

6. The scope of the privilege against incrimination is partially restricted by two statutes:

   (a) s31(1) Theft Act 1968 provides that a witness may not refuse to answer questions in proceedings for the recovery of property or the execution of a trust on the grounds that his answer might lay him open to a charge under the Act;

   (b) s2 Criminal Justice Act 1987 allows the Serious Fraud Squad to compel a person to answer questions in the context of a serious fraud inquiry.

7. Under both s31(1) Theft Act 1968 and s2 Criminal Justice Act 1987, the restriction to the privilege is partial, since answers obtained by compulsion are not admissible in subsequent criminal proceedings.

8. By virtue of a number of other statutes, including the Companies Act 1985, such answers were admissible in subsequent criminal proceedings.

14.4.1 Self-incrimination and human rights

1. In *Saunders v UK* (1997) the ECtHR found there was a breach of Article 6 and stressed that the right not to

incriminate oneself lay at the heart of the concept of a fair trial within article 6.

2. As a result of the *Saunders* decision in the ECtHR, s59 of and Schedule 3 to the Youth Justice and Criminal Evidence Act 1999 amended s434 Companies Act 1985 and a number of other statutes that purported to admit answers compelled during a non-judicial investigation.

3. The present situation seems to be that where the prosecution seeks to rely upon answers obtained from defendants under compulsion at a subsequent criminal trial, judges are obliged to consider the fair trial requirements of Article 6(1), using s78 PACE 1984 to exclude evidence where its admission would adversely affect the fairness of the trial.

4. A number of statutes, including the Road Traffic Act 1988 and legislation in the area of environmental protection, require information to be provided that might be of a self-incriminatory nature.

5. The House of Lords in *R v Hertfordshire CC, ex parte Green Environmental Industries* (2000) applied the following reasoning in holding that there was no violation of Article 6:

   • the provision of information under the relevant statutes creates no presumption of guilt as to the commission of a substantive offence;

   • the court has ample powers to ensure that the proceedings are fair by exercising its discretion to exclude evidence under s78 PACE 1984 where it is unfair to admit it;

   • a request for factual information is lawful even if the answer might be incriminating; it would not be lawful to require a person to make admissions of guilt.

6. Little, if anything, has changed as a result of a further appeal in the *Saunders* case to the Court of Appeal in 2002. The court stressed that statutes that, despite s59 YJCEA 1999, appear to abrogate the privilege against self-incrimination will need to be construed by courts, in the light of Article 6, to determine whether Parliament

intended for evidence gathered in the course of extra-judicial investigations to be admissible at subsequent criminal trials.

14.5 LEGAL PROFESSIONAL PRIVILEGE

1. Legal professional privilege enables confidentiality to be maintained in two types of situation:
   (a) communications between a client and lawyer made for the purpose of obtaining and giving legal advice; and
   (b) communications between a client or his lawyer and third parties (such as potential witnesses and experts) brought into existence in contemplation of a criminal trial or litigation.
2. The rationale behind the privilege was expressed by Lord Taylor CJ in *R v Derby Magistrates' Court, ex parte B* (1996):
   'The principle that runs through [the law] ... is that a man must be able to consult his lawyer in confidence, since otherwise he might hold back half the truth. The client must be sure that what he tells the lawyer in confidence will never be revealed without his consent. Legal professional privilege is thus much more than an ordinary rule of evidence, limited in its application to the facts of a particular case. It is a fundamental condition on which the administration of justice as a whole rests.'
3. To qualify for privileged status:
   (a) communications between client and lawyer must have been confidential in nature, and
   (b) if not actually made in the course of a lawyer/client relationship, must have been made with a view to establishing such a relationship.
4. The privilege extends to instructions by the client to his solicitor and from solicitor to barrister, and covers original documents and copies brought into existence for the purpose of instructing a lawyer.

5. In *Waugh v British Railways Board* (1980) the House of Lords held that in order for communications with third parties to attract privilege, the dominant purpose for the preparation of the reports must have been for submission to a legal adviser for use in litigation.

6. A pre-existing document given into the custody of a solicitor for the purpose of obtaining such advice, or sent to a third party in connection with litigation, is no more privileged than if it remained with the client (*R v Peterborough Justices, ex parte Hicks* (1977); *R v King* (1983)).

14.5.1 Exceptions to the privilege

Privilege can be lost in four ways:

1. **Where advice is sought in furtherance of fraud or some other criminal purpose**.
   (a) The common law rule is illustrated by the old case of *R v Cox & Railton* (1884) and was given statutory force under s10(2) PACE 1984, which provides that 'items held with the intention of furthering a criminal purpose are not items subject to legal privilege'.
   (b) The case of *Francis & Francis v Central Criminal Court* (1988) confirmed that s10(2) was not meant to restrict the common law rule, merely to reinforce it.

2. **Where evidence is necessary to prove innocence, privilege cannot be relied upon.**
   (a) In *R v Barton* (1972) a clerk employed by a firm of solicitors was allowed to adduce 'privileged' documents relating to the affairs of clients in order to further his defence.
   (b) In *R v Ataou* (1988), two co-accused had initially shared the same solicitor, but were separately represented at the time of trial. The trial judge refused to allow Ataou to cross-examine his co-accused on a statement claimed to have been made to his original solicitor in which he exonerated Ataou. The Court of

Appeal held that the burden was on Ataou to show that his interest in seeking to breach the privilege outweighed the interest of his co-accused in maintaining it. The appeal was allowed because the trial judge had failed to apply his mind to balancing the competing interests.

3. **Where secondary evidence is obtained by another party.**

(a) Privilege attaches to conversations between solicitors and clients as well as to documents brought into existence in contemplation of litigation. It attaches to the original document and to copies made for the purpose of instructing a lawyer.

(b) If a document, or a copy of it, falls into the wrong hands, or a privileged conversation is overheard, then the privilege may be lost.

(c) In *R v Tompkins* (1977), an incriminating note from the accused to his counsel was found on the floor of the court and handed to prosecuting counsel. The Court of Appeal upheld the judge's ruling that the prosecution could cross-examine the accused on the matters referred to in the note.

- Where a copy of a privileged document comes into the possession of another party, that party may use the document as secondary evidence.

- The party to whom the privilege attaches may, where the error is discovered at an early stage, seek a court order for the copies to be delivered up and an injunction to restrain the other party from disclosing or making use of the information contained in the document (*Guinness Peat Properties Ltd v Fitzroy Robinson Partnership* (1987)).

- *Lord Ashburton v Pape* (1913) illustrates that where copies of privileged correspondence are obtained by means of a trick, the court will be more than willing to grant an injunction.

4. **Where privilege is waived.**

(a) The party entitled to claim it can always waive

privilege, but once waived, it cannot then be reasserted in relation to that communication/document.

(b) If part of a privileged document is put in evidence, the other party can require the whole document to be disclosed, so waiver of part of a document loses privilege in respect of the entire contents.

14.6 'WITHOUT PREJUDICE' NEGOTIATIONS

1. Communications between opposing parties to litigation or their solicitors do not normally attract legal professional privilege. Because of that risk, privilege does attach to statements made 'without prejudice', i.e. without prejudice to the maker if the terms he proposes are not accepted.

2. If negotiations succeed and a settlement is reached, the without prejudice correspondence remains privileged.

3. Such correspondence is inadmissible in subsequent litigation on the same subject matter, whether between the same or different parties. This rule remains intact following the introduction of the Civil Procedure Rules since one of the major aims of the reforms was to encourage negotiation between disputing parties in an attempt to produce early settlements and avoid litigation.

4. The privilege is the joint privilege of both parties, and extends to their solicitors. It can only be waived with the consent of both parties.

5. The privilege attaches to any discussions or correspondence between actual or prospective parties with a view to avoiding litigation, even where the term 'without prejudice' is not expressly used (*Rush & Tompkins v Greater London Council* (1989)).

14.6.1 Exceptions

1. Without prejudice material is admissible if the issue between the parties at trial is whether or not the

negotiations resulted in an agreed settlement.

2. Each party may agree that a without prejudice document should be disclosed to the court.

3. Without prejudice negotiations may be disclosed where they have been used as a vehicle for fraud.

14.7 EXCLUSION OF EVIDENCE ON THE GROUND OF PUBLIC POLICY (PUBLIC INTEREST IMMUNITY)

Despite the general rule that all relevant evidence is admissible and subject to the rules on disclosure, a direct conflict may sometimes arise between the interests of the state in non-disclosure and the interests of justice and those of the defendant or party to a civil action in disclosing all relevant evidence.

1. In criminal cases, claims for the exclusion of evidence on the ground of Public Interest Immunity (PII) are recognised under s21(2) Criminal Procedure and Investigations Act 1996.

   (a) The Act requires full prosecution disclosure subject to the common law rules on public interest immunity (PII).

   (b) PII is most commonly claimed by Ministers, civil servants or the police, but can also be claimed by other bodies, for example the NSPCC (see *D v NSPCC* (1978); *R v Reading Justices, ex parte Berkshire County Council* (1996) and *R v Brushett* (2001)).

2. Traditionally, PII was claimed either because the nature of a specific document is sensitive (a contents claim) or because a document falls into a class of documents, the whole class of which should be excluded in the public interest (a class claim).

3. Historically, the courts adopted the notion that a mere claim of public interest immunity by a minister in respect

of any document was conclusive (*Duncan v Cammell Laird & Co. Ltd* (1942)).

4. A different approach was adopted in *Conway v Rimmer* (1968), which was historic for two reasons:

   (i) it was the first case in which the House of Lords made use of Lord Gardiner's Practice Statement of 1966 by departing from a previous House of Lords decision;

   (ii) it was the first occasion that a claim of public interest immunity by a Minister was not upheld. Their Lordships held that it was for the trial judge, not the Minister, to decide whether or not to order disclosure where a claim of public interest immunity was made.

5. However, in *Conway v Rimmer* Lord Reid acknowledged that certain classes of document, such as Cabinet papers, ought never to be disclosed unless of historical interest only.

6. In civil cases judges must perform a balancing exercise between the competing interests:

   (a) on the one hand is the public interest in the administration of justice that requires all relevant evidence to be disclosed at trial;

   (b) weighed against that important interest is the need to protect sensitive information that might be damaging either to national security or individuals.

7. In criminal cases the situation is less clear. Following publication of the Scott Report in 1996, Government Ministers are no longer able to claim PII in respect of class claims. The House of Lords in *R v Chief Constable of the West Midlands Police, ex parte Wiley* (1995) suggested that persons or bodies holding sensitive information should conduct an initial balancing exercise to determine whether disclosure was possible, despite the sensitive nature of the documents.

8. In *R v Governor of Pentonville Prison, ex parte Osman (No. 1)* (1992) it was emphasised that a different balancing exercise is required in criminal cases: the weight to be attached to the interests of justice in disclosing all relevant evidence in

a criminal case touching upon and concerning liberty, 'is very great indeed'. This was not a new sentiment: indeed in *Marks v Beyfus* (1890) a very similar view was expressed by Lord Esher MR.

9. *Marks v Beyfus* concerned evidence furnished by a police informer, and this is an area where the scales will normally tip in favour of non-disclosure. The public interest in encouraging people to provide information on criminal activities is itself worthy of protection, thus the burden lies with the defence to show that disclosure of an informer's identity is necessary to the proper presentation of a defence at trial (*R v Hennessey* (1968)).

10. Lord Taylor CJ in *R v Keane* (1994) emphasised that: 'If the disputed material may prove the accused's innocence or avoid a miscarriage of justice, then the balance comes down resoundingly in favour of disclosing it.'

11. A similar public policy exception to the general rule that all relevant evidence must be disclosed exists by virtue of s17(1) and (2) Interception of Communications Act 2000.

    (a) Section 5 of the Act allows for the interception of communications 'for the purpose of preventing or detecting serious crime', subject to the issue of an authorising warrant by the Home Secretary.

    (b) Section 17(1) and (2) prevents the disclosure of any evidence relating to the methods and sources of intercepted information.

12. At first sight this appears to breach Article 6 ECHR. If intercepted evidence were used by the prosecution, yet the defendant, by virtue of s17, were prevented from testing that evidence by questioning the methods by which it was obtained that must restrict his right to a fair trial. The clear view of Lord Hope in *Morgans v DPP* (2001) was that, given the human rights implications which would arise in that situation, evidence obtained by means of intercepted communications 'will always be inadmissible'.

14.8 PUBLIC INTEREST IMMUNITY AND HUMAN RIGHTS

1. The position of the ECtHR in criminal cases is that the prosecution has a duty to disclose any evidence in their possession that might assist an accused in establishing his innocence or obtaining a reduction in sentence.

2. This stance was demonstrated by the Court in *Rowe v UK* (2000):

   'It is a fundamental aspect of the right to a fair trial that criminal proceedings ... should be adversarial and that there should be equality of arms between the prosecution and defence. The right to an adversarial trial means, in a criminal case, that both prosecution and defence must be given the opportunity to have knowledge of and comment on the observations filed and the evidence adduced by the other party.'

3. Importantly, the Court did acknowledge in the same case, that it may sometimes be necessary 'to withhold certain evidence from the defence so as to preserve the fundamental rights of another individual or to safeguard an important public interest'.

4. Despite some important judicial pronouncements, and a general recognition that in criminal cases, the use of PII must be strictly limited, the recent trial of Paul Burrell, former butler to the Princess of Wales, demonstrated that PII is still being used to withhold evidence in criminal trials. The Human Rights Act 1998 should ensure some interesting challenges in the future.

INDEX